The Garden Lover's Guide to the South

PRINCETON ARCHITECTURAL PRESS   NEW YORK

PAUL BENNETT

The Garden Lover's Guide to the South

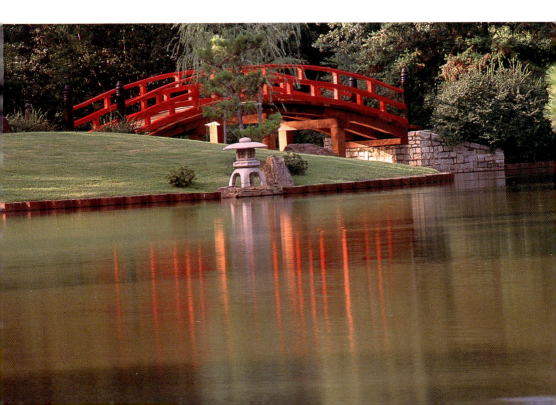

Princeton Architectural Press
37 East 7th Street
New York, NY 10003
212.995.9620

For a free catalog of other books published by Princeton Architectural Press, call toll free 800.722.6657 or visit www.papress.com

All rights reserved.
Text copyright © 2000 Paul Bennett
Cover and book design copyright © 2000 Princeton Architectural Press

No part of this work may be used or reproduced in any manner without written permission from the publisher except in the context of reviews.

Every reasonable attempt has been made to identify owners of copyright. Errors or omissions will be corrected in subsequent editions.

EDITING: Jan Cigliano
DESIGN: Sara E. Stemen
LAYOUT: Adam B. Bohannon
MAPS: Jane Garvie
Special thanks to Ann Alter, Eugenia Bell, Caroline Green, Beth Harrison, Mia Ihara, Clare Jacobson, Leslie Ann Kent, Mark Lamster, Anne Nitschke, Lottchen Shivers, Jennifer Thompson, and Deb Wood of Princeton Architectural Press

—Kevin C. Lippert, *publisher*

Library of Congress Cataloguing-in-Publication Data
Bennett, Paul, 1970–
    Garden lover's guide to the south / by Paul Bennett
        p. cm.
    Includes index.
    ISBN 1-56898-164-3(pbk.: alk. paper)
    1. Gardens—Southern States—Guidebooks. 2. Southern—
    Guidebooks. I. Title.
SB466.U65 S63 2000
712'.0975—dc21

99-059482
CIP

PRINTED IN CHINA
04 03 02 01 00   5 4 3 2 1
FIRST EDITION

Contents

vi	How to use this book
vii	Foreword
viii	Introduction to Southern Gardens
1	Virginia
24	Tobacco Country: *North Carolina, Kentucky, Tennessee*
54	Deep South: *South Carolina, Georgia, Alabama*
88	The Delta: *Arkansas, Mississippi, Louisiana*
110	Florida
130	Texas
145	Biographies
146	Index
148	Acknowledgments and photograph credits

How to use this book

This guide is written for travelers who wish to visit the most historic and beautiful gardens in the southern United States, from the English cottage style gardens of Biltmore in North Carolina and Colonial Williamsburg in Virginia, to the bucolic gardens of the Delta region at Middleton Place in South Caroline and Afton Villa in Louisiana.

The book is divided into six chapters covering the major states of the South. Each chapter comprises an introductory section with a regional map and a list of the gardens, followed by entries on each garden. The numbers found on the regional maps can be used to locate the numbered entries within the chapters. These entries are accompanied by detailed at-a-glance information telling the reader about the garden's main characteristics and nearby sights of interest. The guide also includes five major gardens, beautifully illustrated by three-dimensional plans.

KEY TO SYMBOLS

- Refreshments in vicinity
- Formal garden
- Landscape garden
- House major feature
- Historic garden
- Kitchen garden
- Botanic interest/rare plants
- Topiary
- Borders
- Water features
- Architectural features

Regional maps show locations of gardens.

Each regional map includes a numbered key to make finding garden entries easy.

Entries begin with at-a-glance information on opening times, directions, nearby sights of interest, and how to receive further information.

Major gardens include watercolor plans that note special features.

vi

Foreword

I love gardens not because they're beautiful or because I'm interested in plants, but because they reflect culture. One of the best ways to understand a people is to look at their landscapes, for this is where ideas of power, structure, idealism, and values are expressed within a common language. One of the most enthralling papers I've ever read was an analysis of André Le Nôtre's design for a puzzle garden at Versailles. The garden, which now exists only on paper, was a typical hedge maze with sculptural figures depicting popular fables at various turns. The literal narrative was set up so that if you understood the fables they would point you in the right direction. But a subtext also existed, one in which the designer was subtly—but perceptibly to his intended audience—making a statement about the moral value of the working class and the growing decrepitude of the aristocracy. It was a radical assertion, as Le Nôtre was criticizing his patrons. Not surprisingly the garden was later destroyed.

There are many such subtexts in gardens. Although few are as overtly socialist as Le Nôtre's, there are many equally important issues discussed in today's modern gardens that we should be aware of. The South, of course, is rife with such gardens. As rich a landscape of meaning and symbolism is hard to find on this continent. During out tour, we will observe the fascinating mixture of pastoralism, democracy, and racism embodied in the plantation landscape. We'll also see the overlay of colonial revival and the rise of the theme park garden. And finally, as we creep past the end of the twentieth century, we will find an emergent emphasis on native plants and ecological gardening—a response to contemporary pressures and an indicator of the future.

All of these stories are told, to greater or lesser degree and with greater or lesser artfulness, across the southern landscapes, from the tropics of Florida to the Tobacco fields of Virginia to the dust of Texas. It's a long, strange trip, but one worth taking.

Introduction to Southern Gardens

Unlike the other garden regions of the United States that I've written about—the Northeast and the Midwest—the South is the one place that people automatically associate with a gardening culture. After the Civil War, it is the first thing that pops into people's minds when you mention the South. In some ways this is due to the Civil War, and the image that most people conjure of the typical southern garden is the antebellum plantation. These great plantations were as much working farms as they were expressions of grandeur and greatness carved into the landscape. Like the European aristocracy, southern landowners used design to symbolize and project a sense of power. The big difference with European estates lies in the fact that while European gardens were most always exercises in human control over nature, the South has traditionally maintained a far more ambiguous relationship with nature. In the palatial residential artscapes of the plantations—I'm thinking here particularly of Magnolia Plantation and Middleton Place in South Carolina—the dark, ominous presence of wild nature is always close at hand. In fact it is celebrated to a certain extent, and held as a point of pride. The novels of William Faulkner come to mind, in which the wilderness becomes a kind of character. Man may tame a few acres with crops or a garden, but the boundaries are always near. There's always that verdant and palpably dynamic force just beyond the fence row. In the North nature hibernates. In the winterless south, it is continuously alive.

For the purposes of this book (and those in the series before it), I've defined the South as beginning just beyond the confines of Washington, D.C., in the suburbs of Alexandria. My intent is twofold. It allows me simply to write about all of the gardens in Virginia without making hazy distinctions. But it is also a strategy for understanding an impending battle shaping up in the region. It is a common assumption that the South is a generally rural place, devoid of the industrial problems that plague the cities of the North. This, of course, has not been true for some time. The cities of the South have always been vibrant places, and in the last twenty years have exploded economically. The main side effect of this rapid urbanization has been the engulfing sprawl of suburbs. Those areas around Washington and Atlanta, in particular, are now endless seas of malls and residential developments. The sad irony is that for many years this land immediately outside the city was some of the most beautiful and pristine in the country. We see this all over the South. Outside of Washington there is the Winkler Preserve, outside of Atlanta the Fernbank Science Center, in poor little Key West (condominium capital) Nancy Forrester's noble stand, and the list goes on.

OPPOSITE: *An open landscape expresses the idealism of Edward Bok at Bok Towers in Florida.*

More deeply we see this battle shaping up within existing gardens as an awareness of native plants and ecology takes root. This development is not contained solely within the South, but is spreading throughout the country. In fact if there is a single "cutting edge" trend in garden design today, it's not the "new American garden" (which is just a rehash of English cottage garden style) but a heightened awareness of the traditional garden's complicity in our environmental problems. Complicity? Yes. Gardens are terrible consumers of herbicides and water resources. Grass is called green asphalt by sustainable designers for its tendency to accelerate rain water, which then erodes streams. Traditional gardens are also entry portals for all sorts of exotics and invasives that have scoured our countryside, reducing biodiversity to a few ornamentals and a host of weeds. Of course this is all pretty touchy stuff. Like anything else there are political minefields here planted by fairly radical elements on each side. But what cannot be denied is that people are thinking about these issues, and in the process radically rethinking the garden. We now see gardens that focus on composting, or gardens that use wildflowers and native trees to create landscape experience, xeriscape gardens that demonstrate low herbicide and low water consumption.

In the South the ecological garden revolution is having its greatest impact in the use of native plants. All sorts of gardens, from public botanical gardens with a strong public education focus to estate gardens with a more artistic and historical focus, are cultivating patches of native plants. And people like it. Garden curators all across the region say that these sections within their gardens are the most heavily visited. And the more they are designed to teach lessons, such as how a typical homeowner might use native plants instead of run-of-the-mill exotics, the more successful they are. Some have suggested that this interest indicates a pervasive awareness of the environment in society at large. This is undoubtedly true. But there is also a tinge of patriotism or regionalism in the trend. Native plants, after all, are *of* a place. They are native to somewhere specific. In the South this fact wields particular power.

It strikes at the heartstrings of reconstruction with the promise that finally, after so long, the true South will rise again. But in this iteration, "true South" is a pre-European contact landscape. The native plant gardens of Georgia and South Carolina and elsewhere are not re-creating the mythos of plantation society, but something farther back and deeper—the raw and pristine seventeenth-century landscape that greeted the first settlers. Such an idea of purity is alluring to any

people—even more so to one that has struggled so long to "reconstruct" itself.

The diversity of landscapes across the South makes these kinds of generalizations tenuous. This book lumps gardens in Florida with those in Texas, estates in Virginia with plantations in Louisiana. The Ladybird Johnson Wildflower Center in Austin has lead the way in native plants and ecological gardening for decades, and so it connects nicely with this theme—and the botanical gardens that dot the rest of eastern Texas (the western portion of the state is fairly neglected) are responding in kind. But Florida, to single out one region, presents an entirely different game. This state has always stood apart, with allegiance (at least botanically) to the Caribbean more than to Georgia. The history of Florida is also quite distinct from the rest of the South. We find here some of the best botanical gardens in the country, including the Marie Selby Gardens, as well as the curious idea of the garden as theme park, embodied most fully by Cypress Gardens.

Traditions are still alive in the South, and there are plenty of classic storybook gardens that evoke a *Gone With the Wind* sort of South. But the region is on the move in an economic, civic, and urban sense. And social change has inevitably found its expression in the landscape. It is mind-boggling to consider the region as a whole, and no one can visit all of the gardens. But perhaps if we did we might understand a little bit better the fundamental issues that face the region as well as the country at large.

ABOVE: *Bees are still kept on the grounds at Agecroft in Richmond, Virginia.*

BELOW: *Recent trends in native plantings have found their way to the Norfolk Botanical Garden in Virginia.*

1 Leesburg: Oatlands Plantation	6 Lorton: Gunston Hall	11 Richmond: Agecroft Hall
2 Alexandria: Winkler Botanical Preservation	7 Charlottesville: University of Virginia	12 Richmond: Virginia House
3 Alexandria: Green Spring Gardens Park	8 Charlottesville: Monticello	13 Richmond: Maymont
4 Alexandria: River Farm	9 Lexington: Boxerwood Gardens	14 Williamsburg: Colonial Williamsburg
5 Mount Vernon: Mount Vernon Estate	10 Stratford: Stratford Hall	15 Norfolk: Norfolk Botanical Gardens

VIRGINIA

The northernmost states of the south, like all borderlands, have always had an ambiguous existence. Are they truly southern, wonder their compatriots in Alabama and Mississippi? Doesn't Washington, D.C., epitomize an uptight, amoral northern city more than a context-rich southern metropolis? Like many geographic boundaries that lack a mountain range or coastline to give them definition, the transition from the American North to the American South happens subtly, sometimes imperceptibly. As we drive out of the District of Columbia, we try vainly to sense the borderline between North and South. Surely it is not the Mason–Dixon line, well north of Washington at the Pennsylvania–Maryland border. Is it there in the first line of live oaks? Or is it where the Potomac seems to meander with just a little more style?

It may be an artificial division, but for this book the South begins with Virginia—and Virginia begins with Thomas Jefferson. After two hundred years Jefferson's landscapes at Monticello and the University of Virginia continue to exert an undeniable force on the garden identity of Virginia. At his home at Monticello Jefferson used the landscape to experiment with botanical discoveries brought back from the Lewis and Clark expedition and sent to him by his network of fellow plant collectors, such as George Washington and John Bartram. Monticello was also a spatial palette upon which the "amateur" architect experimented with form. While most historians focus upon the architecture at Monticello and the University of Virginia, in many ways this is the least interesting part of these places, or the least relevant. Architecturally, Jefferson was trying to re-invent the

OPPOSITE: *George Washington's Mount Vernon*

forms of classical Europe within an American context. But the gardens and landscapes break out of the circumscription of history. They are not Italianate or even English (the two landscape traditions most prominent at the time), but wholly original statements that continue to beguile a contemporary mind jaded by so much modernism.

The other major gardens singled out in Virginia are the exceptional museum pieces at Colonial Williamsburg, designed in the 1920s by Arthur Shurcliff and in the 1950s by Alden Hopkins. In many ways Williamsburg was the first theme park—albeit a far more sophisticated one than those we think of today—and its landscape provides a fascinating lens through which to view history. In recent years extensive research has helped designers mirror colonial gardening practices; however the most exhilarating experiences are to be found in the original colonial revival spaces, which reflect Victorian ideas more than any true gardening practices of the eighteenth century. The chapter ends with one of the more lovely public gardens in the country, the Norfolk Botanical Gardens. Although located next to a busy airport, the gardens are embraced by lush azalea woods and miles of freshwater streams. Few more beautiful places are to be found for hundreds of miles.

VIRGINIA

1 Leesburg: Oatlands Plantation

LOCATION: U. S. ROUTE 15, SIX MILES SOUTH OF LEESBURG

GARDEN OPEN: 10:00 am–4:30 pm daily, late March–December. ADMISSION: free.

FURTHER INFORMATION FROM: 20850 Oatlands Plantation Lane, Leesburg 20175
(703) 777-3174

NEARBY SIGHTS OF INTEREST: Harper's Ferry National Historical Park, Manassas National Battlefield Park

With Confederate and Union troops fighting all about this area during the Civil War, it is a miracle that the Oatlands Plantation was spared. Perhaps the greater miracle is that it didn't succumb to the economic hardship that blighted the region after the war, and that it can still be enjoyed today. George Carter, a great-grandson of Robert "King" Carter, built the gracious neoclassical manor house in 1803. A prosperous planter up until the war, Carter transformed the estate into a 3,000-acre working plantation. Washington Brahmins William and Edith Eustis purchased the ailing estate in 1903 and set about transforming Carter's utilitarian landscape into pleasure grounds befitting their stature. Mrs. Eustis created several grand gardens near the house, including a rose garden and a sundial boxwood parterre shrouded beneath a canopy of magnolia and replete with statuary and other architectural ornamentation. The Eustises bequeathed their property to the National Trust for Historic Preservation in 1930, and garden designer Alfredo Siani was hired to reinvigorate the landscape. He restored the flowerbeds to the soft pink and blue hues of Mrs. Eustis' preference. Siani also constructed several gardens to his own tastes, such as the Short Terraces of hot yellows and reds. The sequential layout of the gardens is best measured from the balustrade that separates the lawn of the house from the garden. Here one gets the most profound sense of the subtlety of Virginia plantation design.

OPPOSITE: *Maymont's arbor*
BELOW: *The balustrade separates the house lawn from the garden.*

VIRGINIA

GARDENS OPEN: 7:30 am–3:00 pm Monday–Friday. ADMISSION: free.

FURTHER INFORMATION FROM:
5400 Roanoke Avenue,
Alexandria 22311
(703) 578-9109

NEARBY SIGHTS OF INTEREST:
Arlington National Cemetery

The natural beauty of the northern Virginia landscape is preserved at Winkler Botanical Preserve.

2 Alexandria: Winkler Botanical Preserve

LOCATION: ROANOKE STREET, OFF BEAUREGARD, EXIT 4 OF I-395, FOUR MILES SOUTH OF WASHINGTON, D.C.

There is little open space left in northern Virginia, a region that everyday gives new definition to the word "sprawl." In response to the inexorable progression of the suburbs the Winkler Preserve was established in 1980s. The garden is a naturalistic botanical preserve that focuses on species native to the Potomac River region. Woodland trails wind through forty-three acres of reclaimed land that was once a dumping ground and a pig farm. Those days are long past thanks to careful forest management and the planting of thousands of native shrubs and wildflowers. Most of the collection of Virginia bluebells, alder, violets, and larkspur was rescued from other sites in the area. In the spring the floral displays come alive beneath a tapestry of mixed oaks and chestnuts. A highlight of the garden is a wetland meadow planted with goldenrod and coneflower. Hidden within the vegetation are a series of check dams that carefully regulate the water volume in several catch basins. As the surrounding area becomes more developed stormwater runoff into the preserve has increased. And the meadow garden provides a smart (and beautiful) way to mitigate this consequence. The twenty-five-foot waterfall and abundant plantings also serve to improve water quality. The peace and calm of the scene is always kept in perspective by the hum of the highway nearby, an appropriate and critical component of the garden experience.

3 Alexandria: Green Spring Gardens Park

LOCATION: LITTLE RIVER TURNPIKE, NEAR ANNANDALE, EIGHT MILES SOUTH OF WASHINGTON

GARDEN OPEN: dawn–dusk daily. ADMISSION: free.

FURTHER INFORMATION FROM:
4603 Green Spring Road
Alexandria 22312
(703) 642-5173

NEARBY SIGHTS OF INTEREST:
Meadowlark Gardens Regional Park, Winkler Botanical Preserve

The last owners of this 1760 manor house in the far reaches of Alexandria were good friends with Beatrix Farrand and in the 1940s hired the garden designer to create the landscape around this home as well as those at their estate on Long Island. Farrand sketched the bones of the design, but it has evolved considerably over the years under the guidance of the county parks association that manages the property today. Public demonstration gardens are now the *modus operandi* at Green Spring, including townhouse gardens that communicate ideas for planting a small, often shady area, and several border gardens. During the later years of her career Farrand conducted a close study of Gertrude Jekyll, and began designing linear spaces in that vein. A blue border of delphiniums, lobelia, and other azure combinations that leads down a slope to a gazebo gives us hints of this direction, while a mixed border of perennials in an interwoven pastiche works in an entirely different direction from Jekyll's signature "clumping." Elsewhere the gardens around the manor include a shade garden, a rock garden, an orchard of pears and apples (some of which are espaliered), and a native plant garden featuring common northern Virginian varieties, such as Virginia bluebells and trillium.

A border of mixed perennials leads to the gazebo.

4 Alexandria: River Farm

LOCATION: OFF MOUNT VERNON MEMORIAL PARKWAY, SEVEN MILES SOUTH OF WASHINGTON, D.C.

GARDEN OPEN: 8:30 am–5:00 pm daily, except holidays.
ADMISSION: free

FURTHER INFORMATION FROM:
7931 East Boulevard Drive,
Alexandria, VA 22308
(703) 768-5700
www.ahs.org

NEARBY SIGHTS OF INTEREST:
Old Town Alexandria,
Arlington National Cemetery

By 1787 George Washington's acquisition spree along the Potomac River extended to five different farms, totaling nearly 8,000 acres. River Farm, now separated by several subdivisions from Mount Vernon, was the farthest reach of the property. Although it passed to successive generations of Washingtons, by the twentieth century the property was experiencing hard times. In the 1970s, a desperate owner even courted the Soviet Union as a potential buyer (Moscow considered establishing an embassy here), which outraged many patriotic souls, including Enid Annenberg Haupt, patron of the New York Botanical Garden and board member of the American Horticultural Society. She purchased the property in 1973 and donated it to the Society, which now uses it as its administrative base and cultivates several gardens onsite. In front of the 1757 brick house there are several collections of dogwoods, azaleas, and fruit trees, and a *Front Yard Garden* that showcases common American yard plants. Behind the house there are more formal gardens, many of which are sponsored by plant organizations, including a rose garden, a perennial border, and an herb garden laid out in a radial manner with peach trees anchoring each bed. A heavy wisteria arbor lines the far end of the property. A children's garden designed by different school groups in conjunction with professional landscape architects, horticulturists, and nurseries proves the most eye-catching from afar. The garish competes with the interesting in this visually eclectic space with the most evocative contribution being the very simple, very beautiful *Native Plant Butterfly Garden*, featuring rue, hollyhocks, and milkweed. While the rest of River Farm, surprisingly, lacks extensive plant labeling, this area is fairly well-interpreted and should prove educational for children. The vistas of the Potomac River are more striking at Mount Vernon, Washington's better-known property downstream. At the edge of the sloping lawn is a *Wildlife Garden* planted with coneflower to attract butterflies and designed around a small pond, tucked into a copse of trees like a grotto. The most attractive garden at River Farm is immediately behind the house in the *Garden Calm,* an enclosed room of shady plants presided over by a 200-year-old osage orange tree.

George Washington's River Farm retains a rustic character.

VIRGINIA

5 Mount Vernon: Mount Vernon Estate

LOCATION: MOUNT VERNON MEMORIAL PARKWAY (STATE ROUTE 400), TEN MILES SOUTH OF WASHINGTON, D.C.

GARDEN OPEN: 8 am–5 pm, April–August; 9 am–5 pm, March, September, and October; 9 am–4 pm, November–February. ADMISSION: $8.00.

FURTHER INFORMATION FROM: Mount Vernon Memorial Parkway, Mount Vernon 22121 (703) 780-2000

NEARBY SIGHTS OF INTEREST: Old Town Alexandria, Arlington National Cemetery

By the end of the Revolutionary War George Washington was as close to an American saint as the country would ever produce. While his national popularity would eventually forced him back into public life, his first thoughts after the end of the war were of his estate along the Potomac River and farming. In imitation of his fellow Virginians, Washington first planted tobacco at Mount Vernon, which he farmed with an army of three hundred slaves. But the temperamental plant disliked the clay soil, and Washington found he could not compete with the more productive plantations farther south. This economic circumstance caused him to investigate other, innovative agricultural options—wheat, flax, and hemp—and spurred his naturally inquisitive nature to seek out European tracts on the "new husbandry" by such writers as Arthur Young, Jethro Tull, and Duhamel de Monceau. As a young man Washington worked as a land surveyor in Northern Virginia, and when he moved to Mount Vernon one of the first things he did was layout the landscape in such a way as to accommodate his agricultural pursuits with other less utilitarian uses. Around the house are formal lawns that give vistas of the Potomac as well as a central *Bowling Green* lined with enormous tulip poplars that frame the house from the approaching circular drive. Extending down the slope Washington experimented with seeds gathered from friends and planted an arboretum of locusts and crabapples that roll toward the fields.

Careful restoration has brought to life George Washington's gardens.

In addition to landscape architecture, Washington was an avid gardener. In the *Lower Garden*, or *Kitchen Garden*, located south of the Bowling Green, vegetables and fruit were planted in square beds cut through the middle by a single allée of naturalistic boxwood. Downslope, this formal but unadorned geometry is continued, with the exception of a radial herb garden, and framed in brick. The sunken beds are still planted with vegetables and herbs, many of which were common in the eighteenth century and recorded in the letters and diaries of Washington himself. However they are roped off to visitors. The gnarled and overgrown boxwood dates to Washington's time. In the upper half of the garden the beds are now planted with flowering perennials and annuals, including peonies and foxglove. A handsome brick wall lined with espaliered fruit trees forms the northern border, while a hedge and white fence progress to an octagonal summer house along the east. To the south a sunny view opens over fields and country lanes.

On the opposite side of the bowling green the upper garden mirrors the lower garden in design. However the beds contain a dynamic display of well-labeled perennials that include coneflower and poppy set amid carpets of lamb's ear, all flutteringly alive with butterflies. Originally this too was a working garden, but Washington transformed it into a pleasure garden in 1785. The diversity of plants reflects Washington's own tastes, which were often encouraged by friends and colleagues who sent him exotic seeds and cuttings. The last formal garden at Mount Vernon is the diminutive *Botanical Garden*, located just outside the walls of the upper garden. Although not much to look at, this is where Washington experimented with horticultural varieties. Today the garden is sown each year with a different plant to reflect how it would have appeared two hundred years ago.

6 Lorton: Gunston Hall

LOCATION: MASON NECK, FIFTEEN MILES SOUTH OF WASHINGTON, D.C., ON MOUNT VERNON HIGHWAY

GARDEN AND HOUSE OPEN: 9:30 am–5:00 pm daily, except Thanksgiving, Christmas, and New Year's Day. ADMISSION: $5.

FURTHER INFORMATION FROM: Gunston Hall Plantation, Mason Neck 22079 (703) 550-9220

NEARBY SIGHTS OF INTEREST: Mount Vernon

The force of George Mason's strong-willed personality was very much felt in that famous Philadelphia meeting hall in the summer of 1787, although in the end this enigmatic Virginian refused to vote in favor of the new federal Constitution because it did not include a bill of rights. Mason's ideas of rights, and his very language used to describe them in the adamant Virginia Declaration of Rights, influenced both the Declaration of Independence and the Bill of Rights, when the latter was finally drawn up in 1791.

Mason's actions would have assured him expulsion from modern day politics, and perhaps from the eighteenth century's as well, if he hadn't opted for the private life of his own accord. He was, first and foremost, a gentleman farmer. Like his neighbor George Washington, Mason believed that working the land elevated the human spirit and contributed not only to one's well-being but also to one's liberty. Gunston Hall, Mason's wheat and tobacco plantation and home on the Potomac River, is the physical manifestation of these ideas. Built in 1775, the house contains many period furnishings, some of which belonged to Mason and his descendants, and some of which were brought in from elsewhere. Of the original 5,500 acres of croplands, forest, and gardens that once surrounded the house, 500 remain, including many outbuildings and garden areas. The house is approached through a stately allée of magnolia, shrouded from the wind by an outer row of arborvitae. Built by a subsequent owner, in form it echoes an original allée of cherry trees planted and admired by Mason, which serves to create a dramatic approach to the Georgian manor house. Behind the house lie the formal gardens. The overgrown, aromatic boxwood allée that splits the area (and mirrors the allée in the front) was planted by Mason, however the surrounding plantings were designed by Alden Hopkins, a landscape architect at Colonial Williamsburg, in the 1950s when the museum first opened. Hopkins' interpretation is widely regarded as beautiful but far more indicative of the colonial revival style than anything Mason would have planted. Victorian parterres filled with perennials and cutting a striking geometry from the lawn were probably not in Mason's decidedly rural, no-nonsense vocabulary. For a few years debate centered around whether to preserve Alden's design (a shining example of the colonial revival style) or to excavate the garden in an effort to reveal what Mason's original garden might have looked like. The decision was made to excavate. As a result the landscape is fairly unattractive (temporarily), although highly interesting. Expect much fascinating information to be gleaned about the garden through the modern archeological techniques being applied to the site.

A smaller, sunken garden—also designed by Hopkins—remains at the edge of the property. The woods beyond this and separating the house from the river were fenced off as a deer park in Mason's day. Around the side of the house there are several herb and vegetable gardens planted with authentic colonial varieties, although they are not labeled. The slave quarters—and Mason owned many slaves—were located near the kitchen garden. The foundation of one structure remains intact, a tiny, windowless building that would have housed two families and serves as an important counterpoint to Mason's ideas greatest legacy,the preamble, "That all men are by nature equally free and independent."

The lower parterre garden at Gunston Hall overlooks George Mason's deer park.

VIRGINIA

GARDENS OPEN: dawn to dusk daily. **ADMISSION:** free.

FURTHER INFORMATION FROM:
P.O. Box 9017, Charlottesville 22906
(804) 924-7751
www.uva.edu

NEARBY SIGHTS OF INTEREST:
Monticello, Ash Lawn, downtown Charlottesville

7 Charlottesville: University of Virginia pavilion gardens

LOCATION: UNIVERSITY AVENUE, BEHIND THE ROTUNDA, CHARLOTTESVILLE

If Thomas Jefferson was a notable architect he was a revolutionary landscape architect. The University of Virginia, which Jefferson planned in 1816, is a masterpiece of spatial organization. Jefferson's intent was to create what he called an academical village of pavilions, each designed in a different architectural style and linked by an arcade. The unifying structure is a series of cascading lawns that elegantly step down over a course of almost a hundred yards. Although the magnificent Rotunda, which housed the library, dominated the architecture and hence the symbolism of the academical village, the Lawn in its perfect proportion and geometrical simplicity, embodied the moral values Jefferson meant to instill in the youth of Virginia.

Behind the pavilions, which continue to house faculty and students, are a series of residential-sized gardens. An unusual serpentine wall outlines each plot. This is Jefferson's only imprint on the actual gardens, as he died before they were laid out. For most of their history each garden was designed by the families that lived in the pavilions, but in the 1960s the Garden Club of Virginia asked Alden Hopkins, then chief landscape architect at Colonial Williamsburg, to create a "Jeffersonian" design for each. His main idea was to design subtle spaces with minimal gestures: a single path, a couple of large shade trees, greenswards, simple beds, and such. In spirit Hopkins was thinking of Jefferson's own designs at Monticello, but also about what Jefferson might have recommended for a more public place. The gardens continue to serve those who live in the pavilions, and are mostly open to the public. The rule is, leave gates open when you find them, closed when you find them, and don't intrude if there is any sign to that effect.

The neoclassical pavilion gardens at the University of Virginia—perfect for students' repose

VIRGINIA

8 Charlottesville: Monticello

LOCATION: STATE ROUTE 53, TWO MILES SOUTHEAST OF CHARLOTTESVILLE

For some, the greatest contribution Thomas Jefferson made to American culture was to infuse into it a healthy does of European traditions. One such tradition was the view that gardens were a fine art and landscape architecture a necessary component to civilization-building. On a journey to France in 1788 Jefferson wrote that Americans should imitate the gardens of that country because they were at once nobly conceived and inexpensive to create. "We have only to cut out the superabundant plants," the ever pragmatic Jefferson added. More evidence of his high estimation of gardening can be gleaned from a later letter on establishing the University of Virginia, in which he included gardening alongside architecture, painting, sculpture, and music as essential to education.

Upon visiting Jefferson's home at Monticello, however, one needs few such expository sources to grasp how highly Jefferson regarded the design arts. Although the neoclassical architecture of the house is impressive, the greater genius lies in how Jefferson sited the building in the landscape. The house sits at the eastern end of a oval-shaped lawn, loosely defined by a meandering path. From the porches of the manor house the lawn underlies excellent views of the uninhabited mountain tops that surrounded his plantation. That they remain devoid of development today is a testament both to Jefferson's foresight—until recently it would have been hard to build upon these steep slopes—and the efforts of contemporary preserva-

GARDENS OPEN: 8:00 am to 5:00 pm, March–October; 9:00 am to 4:30 pm, October–February. ADMISSION: $9 adults, $5 children.

FURTHER INFORMATION FROM:
P. O. Box 217, Charlottesville 22902
(804) 984-9822
www.monticello.org

NEARBY SIGHTS OF INTEREST:
University of Virginia, Ash Lawn

Thomas Jefferson's private residence and gardens—his reprieve from Washington, D.C., as president of the United States, and from Charlottesville, as founder of the University of Virginia

tionists. Although the garden is pleasant when viewed from the house, Jefferson intended this to be a stroll garden (he used the term "roundabout flower garden"). The greater effect is had by walking around its circuit, slowly taking in many varieties of flowers and attractive views of the house across the great lawn. Near to the house are a series of free-standing oval beds that Jefferson planted with single species, while farther away from house, as if in attempt to strengthen the sense of transition from architecture to nature, the beds become mixed, and then wilder in composition.

Jefferson, of course, was an accomplished horticulturist and traded seeds with other plantsmen up and down the eastern seaboard. When he authorized Lewis and Clark to explore the newly purchased Louisiana territory in 1803, one of Jefferson's key requests was for the explorers to gather as many samples of the flora on their journey as possible. While the effect of this preoccupation can be observed to some extent in the flower garden, most of Jefferson's experimentation with plants occurred in his vegetable garden, which occupies a long plot of land just below the crest of hill to the south of the house. Demarcated at its midway point by the handsome Garden Pavilion (a reconstruction dating from 1984), the vegetable garden is still tended by an army of gardeners in much the condition Jefferson once kept it, including such eighteenth-century exotics as tomatoes, sesame, and twenty varieties of peas. The landscape continues to drop off below a retaining wall to a large fruit orchard and small vineyard. Wine-making was one of Jefferson's passions and production is kept up by a viticulturist today. From atop the garden wall are the best unobstructed views of the surrounding hillside, and it is said that this was Jefferson's favorite place in the entire garden.

9 Lexington: Boxerwood Gardens

LOCATION: ROSS ROAD, ABOUT ONE MILE OUTSIDE OF TOWN

GARDENS OPEN: 9 am to 4 pm Thursday–Sunday. **ADMISSION:** $4 donation.

FURTHER INFORMATION FROM:
963 Ross Road, Lexington 24450
(540) 463-2697
www.boxerwood.com

NEARBY SIGHTS OF INTEREST:
Virginia Military Institute

Robert Munger began Boxerwood simply by planting trees on his property in the mountains of Lexington. Over the years—he started in 1956—Munger's property began to evolve into a beautiful arboretum where the existing mature forest is intermixed with a influx of colorful ornamental shrubbery and understory plantings. (The name comes from Munger's love of dogs.) The palette is considered entirely native, or at least those hardy species that can grow here without problem but are not invasive. The beauty of the garden lies in the incredible layers of natural succession. The understory, a layer cake of dogwood, Japanese maples, and redbud, is twenty to forty years old, and hence consists of fairly mature first-growth plant material. The effect is sublime. The filtered light has a cathedral quality; the mixture of textures and colors at times seems painted. Yet Munger's approach was hands-off and the forest remains fairly unmanaged. What we see is the barest of editing, and since his protege Karen "KB" Bailey has been following Munger's lead since his death several years ago, the gardens promise to continue this legacy.

Munger believed that gardening was a dance with nature: sometimes you might lead, but you were never in control. Although he created several notable collections, including those of dwarf conifers, rhododendrons, and azaleas, the garden does not read like a botanical garden. It eschews such overt control, and prefers simply to dance, so to speak.

At times the mature forest of Boxerwood explodes in ecstasy

10 Stratford: Stratford Hall Plantation

LOCATION: STATE ROUTE 214 OUT OF LERTY, ABOUT FORTY-FIVE MILES SOUTHEAST OF FREDERICKSBURG

GARDENS OPEN: 9:00 am to 4:30 pm daily, year-round.
ADMISSION: $7 adults, $6 seniors, $3 children.

FURTHER INFORMATION FROM:
Robert E. Lee Memorial Association, Stratford 22558
(804) 493-8038
www.stratfordhall.org

NEARBY SIGHTS OF INTEREST:
George Washington Birthplace National Monument

Thomas Lee, a wealthy land speculator, carved Stratford Hall from the wilderness in the 1730s. The plantation thrived for a hundred years on tobacco, and saw a succession of Lees pass through its confines—magistrates of Virginia, signers of the Declaration of Independence, and finally Robert E. Lee, general of the Confederate Army during the Civil War. In the 1930s a nonprofit foundation sought to restore the historic house and grounds. To this end they hired Arthur Shurcliff, whom John D. Rockefeller Jr., had employed to build his museum at Colonial Williamsburg. Shurcliff designed the East Garden based partly on research of old records, archaeology, and oral history and partly inspired by the Victorian-influenced colonial revival style. It featured an extensive parterre of boxwood and oyster shell paths. This was simplified in the 1950s by his successor at Williamsburg, Alden Hopkins. The center has been cleared out for a grass panel, and a variety of shrub and flower plantings were instituted, such as crepe myrtle, camellias, and flowering cherries. Just beyond the boundary of boxwood lies a small orchard. The *West Garden* was designed by the New York firm Innocenti and Webel in the 1940s; due to Stratford's lack of funds for this project, it was a twenty-year-old plan when implemented in the 1960s. The garden scheme is basically a radial geometric evolving into a standard rectangular arrangement of flowerbeds farther from the house. Old-fashioned perennials dominate, such as foxglove, coreopsis, and coneflower. A lot of archeological research has

West Garden designed by Innocenti and Webel in the 1940s

been conducted in the gardens and landscape that has uncovered numerous layers of history. The West Garden was discovered to have been a formal garden dating from the early nineteenth century. A small herb garden was also found, and this has recently been restored. On the way to the diminutive slave quarters is a rustic vegetable garden, and there has been much archeological activity here in attempt to understand the undocumented society of plantation slaves. From the north terrace of the house a breathtaking vista opens up, which has been enhanced and cared for through the years—a rather unusual feat in this era of disappearing open space.

11 Richmond: Agecroft Hall

LOCATION: SULGRAVE ROAD, OFF CARY STREET

In the 1920s T. C. Williams embodied the conflicted soul of the South. Born into Richmond's landed gentry, Williams acted in the true spirit of a northern capitalist when he carved up his family estate, Windsor, to create the fashionable development on the edge of the city, Windsor Farms. But while Williams and his architect Henry G. Morse constructed standard Richmond manses for the wealthy patrons of the subdivision, for himself the developer journeyed to Lancashire, England, and carted back in innumerable boxes the twelfth-century manor, Agecroft Hall. Williams hired local Richmond landscape architect Charles Gillette to layout the grounds and surround the house with gardens. Because the house went through its most significant architectural development in the seventeenth century, contemporary garden curators are editing Gillette's work slightly to reflect this period as well. For instance, in the forecourt garden Gillette's foundation plantings and ornamental boxwood have been removed in favor of a simpler cobblestone paved plaza and beds of perennials along the outer wall.

A fragrance garden is opportunistically placed beneath the kitchen of the house. Surrounded on all sides by ubiquitous boxwood, an olfactory salad of delphinium, foxglove, and thyme not only fill the air but give the garden a precious atmosphere too. Over a balustrade one looks upon Gillette's *Sunken Garden*. Low walls of aged brick capped with bluestone outline a sharp and handsomely proportioned lawn panel. The borders are planted with hundreds of tulips in early spring that, when they burst forth, strengthen the strong simplicity and visual boldness of the stone and brick. Outside of a dense hedge of American boxwood two allées frame the Sunken Garden. The older and more purely magical is the crepe myrtle allée featuring an array of seventy- and eighty-year-old trees

---

GARDEN OPEN: 10:00 am to 4:00 pm Tuesday–Saturday; 12:30 pm to 5:00 pm Sunday, year-round. ADMISSION: $2.

FURTHER INFORMATION FROM: 4305 Sulgrave Road, Richmond 23221. (804) 353-4241

NEARBY SIGHTS OF INTEREST: Virginia House, Wilton, Hollywood Cemetery

descending down a slight slope. Pollarded little leaf lindens make up the other allée.

At the far end of this northern side of the house the property dips down a short, sharp slope of English ivy interlaced with attractive paths. At the bottom lie three authentic seventeenth-century gardens. The first is an *Elizabethan knot garden*, perfectly designed, constructed, and maintained to give a succinct impression of interwoven strands—like threads or rope. The central garden is dedicated to the two great baroque gardeners, John Tradescant the elder and the younger, both of whom traveled the world in search of exotic plants. The selection here reflects that spirit, but as many of the Tradescants' novelties were Virginian varieties discovered here and brought to England, a significant portion of the garden is given over to native species. The space is well organized, yet minute, so that the eye wanders through this garden unhurriedly. Four outlying beds centered on rounded topiaries structure it, while a network of paths, platforms, potted plants, and architecture create a matrix of interest. The last garden in the series features old varieties of herbs.

From the terrace behind the house are excellent views of the James River. At the southern end of this porch lies the *Romantic Garden*, which is essentially a fountain set within a tight enclosure. A rose walk of heritage climbers leads from here onto the lawn where the gardeners have cut a turf maze and mowed a bowling green, the former supposedly the original incarnation of the form.

The beautiful sunken garden at Agecroft creates a place separate from the house.

VIRGINIA

GARDENS OPEN: 10:00 am to 4:00 pm Tuesday–Saturday; 12:30 pm to 5:00 pm Sunday, year-round. **ADMISSION:** $2.

FURTHER INFORMATION:
4301 Sulgrave Road,
Richmond 23221
(804) 353-4251

NEARBY SIGHTS OF INTEREST:
Agecroft Hall, Wilton

12 Richmond: Virginia House

LOCATION: SULGRAVE ROAD, OFF CARY STREET

It was Alexander and Virginia Weddell who first came up with the idea of importing a relic of English architecture to the woods of Windsor Farms. And although their neighbor T. C. Williams had erected Agecroft Hall several years in earlier, the Weddells took the honors of the ancient—their "Virginia House" was actually a priory dating back to 1119.

The gardens at Virginia House were designed by Charles Gillette, the same landscape architect who designed the grounds at Agecroft. But the two properties could not be more different. There is no strict historical program that guides these gardens other than the pursuit of the beautiful. The working entrance of the house, which today operates as a museum, is situated within a secluded side garden. Overhung by a pleasant canopy of shade trees, the area evokes quiet contemplation. A chain hung between pedestals supports a line of flowering vines. This form is echoed on the other side by a wooden loggia supported by stone columns. Nestled between these is an intricate matrix of stepping stones and boxwood clipped low. So that the effect is relaxed and informal—dark, understated, calmly southern.

A terrace lines the back of the house, and from here a tight circuit of gardens lays out. Immediately below is the *Canal Garden,* a linear sluice of water lined in stone and planted with bunches of Japanese water iris and sagittaria. Perennials enclose one end while the other proceeds across a fountain plaza and visually ends in a pergola. Small garden areas are arranged around this axis, which soften the architectural arrangement but the focal point remains the sharp canal. The rest of the formal gardens wrap around toward the river on the high ground along the southern edge of the property. Here is a garden of hardy azaleas woven into a small glade. Running parallel is the rose garden, which due to lack of light and air flow has fared poorly since it was planted in the 1940s, followed at its terminus by the perfectly square *Tea Garden*, a diminutive patch of grass, centered upon a small fountain and surrounded by a mixed border. Downhill from these gardens are several landscape gardens, including a meadow of wildflowers and a woodland walk, both of which are awaiting redesign.

The Weddells were lifelong diplomats who, from their posts in South America and Europe, acquired vast collections of paintings, sculpture, furniture, and decorative arts. The eclectic array of the house belies their cosmopolitan spirit while the orderliness of grounds is a testament to their uncompromising good taste.

A circuit of gardens extends from the house's back terrace.

13 Richmond: Maymont

LOCATION: PARK DRIVE, OFF BLANTON, NOT FAR FROM THE MAPLEWOOD EXIT ON INTERSTATE 95, DOWNTOWN

GARDENS OPEN: 10 am to 7 pm daily, April–October; 10 am to 5 pm, November–March. **ADMISSION:** free.

HOUSE OPEN: same as the garden; closed on Monday.

FURTHER INFORMATION FROM: 1700 Hampton Street, Richmond 23220 (804) 358-7166

NEARBY SIGHTS OF INTEREST: Museum of Fine Arts

James Dooley and his wife Sallie May were a late-nineteenth-century success story. The son of Irish immigrants who luckily received an education at Georgetown, Dooley returned to Richmond where his father had prospered as a hat manufacturer and set about making his own fortune, primarily in rebuilding the southern railroads. In 1886 the Dooleys purchased a hundred-acre farm on the James River and set about constructing an estate in perfect Gilded Age splendor. The sandstone house was designed by Edgerton Roberts, a young architect whose only other commission was the Virginia building at the Chicago Exposition of 1893. After the turn of the century the Dooleys hired the landscape architecture firm of Noland and Baskerville to design a romantic landscape in the English country style and an Italian garden near the house. The garden is a perfect example of its type, with majestic balustraded terraces overlooking a flowing design of green boxwood interpenetrated with hints of floral color. A small patch of purple wisteria overwhelms the granite pergola, giving the garden a piquant vibrancy, the strength of which is derived from an excellent restoration completed in the 1980s. A staircase of water, called the Cascade, connects the garden to its lower terrace, and from there into the parklike landscape. In 1910 the Dooleys commissioned Japanese master gardener Muto to create a Japanese garden. The spine of the garden is an intimate watercourse that begins at a stone-encased waterfall and winds around to a small pond. The style is a stroll garden, enhanced by a pleasant walk. Along the way carefully crafted turns in the path focus views on arranged garden scenes, much like in a conservatory but done with a grace and subtlety that is uncommon in western design. The garden suffered from neglect in the 1970s after the property had been deeded to public trust. But restoration and expansion, implemented by landscape architect Barry Starke, has made it one of the chief features of Maymont. Not to be overlooked is the pastoral landscape that surrounds the house and gardens, and which the Dooleys fashioned into an arboretum with many important exotics imported from abroad, including the false larch (*Pseudolarix kaempferi*) and Persian parrotia (*Parrotia persica*). The landscape was designed by John Baskerville, who was well-schooled in the English tradition. The house looks down upon the land that is organized like a tapestry with certain groupings and framed views to provide depth of field and interest. The key to the collection is the fact that at the beginning the Dooleys didn't plant specimens too closely, thus allowing them room to grow into the giants they are today.

A Japanese garden with southern flair graces the grounds at Maymont.

VIRGINIA

GARDENS OPEN: 9:00 am to 5:30 pm daily, year-round.

FURTHER INFORMATION FROM:
Colonial Parkway,
Williamsburg 23187
(800) HIS-TORY

NEARBY SIGHTS OF INTEREST:
College of William and Mary, Jamestown Settlement, Busch Gardens

14 Williamsburg: Colonial Williamsburg

LOCATION: OFF INTERSTATE 64, THIRTY MILES SOUTHEAST OF RICHMOND

When the capital of Virginia was relocated from Williamsburg to Richmond in 1780 it sounded the death knell for this small colonial town. Although some mercantile traffic continued to pass through on its way to and from the ports at Hampton Roads, the hamlet went from the center to the fringe in no time. By the time John D. Rockefeller Jr., laid his eyes on the place in the 1920s it was dilapidated. Perfect, thought Rockefeller. There could be fewer better ways to pay back his debt to the society that made him rich than by bringing back to life this artifact of American democracy.

Williamsburg was the first theme park and period museum in the country. The mastermind behind its creation was Arthur Shurcliff, a Boston landscape architect who had apprenticed with Frederick Law Olmsted. Shurcliff understood Rockefeller's vision and, better than anybody until Walt Disney, also understood how design could make it work. The town as we see it today was carefully reconstructed, restoring those structures that existed on-site at the time, but heavily augmenting them with other historic houses and barns that were brought in from the countryside. An entire program was developed to tell the story of the colonial leaders of Virginia: how they gathered here to debate the heavy issues of the colony, including the formulation of the Virginia constitution and bill of rights. The College of William and Mary anchors one end of

the town—in many ways its most authentic testament to the past—while the rest has become a kind of interpretive landscape, dotted with docents in period garb and tourists from Nebraska, Arizona, and Osaka eating ice-cream cones and imagining the heady days of Jefferson.

    The success of Williamsburg in many ways lies in the fact that it is not authentic at all. The landscape is far less colonial than it is colonial revival—that period at the end of the nineteenth and beginning of the twentieth centuries when the American patriotic spirit turned to the restoration of the past. The aesthetic of Shurcliff and his contemporary garden makers was Victorian, and he used vibrant exotics to make Williamsburg a colorful, wonderfully verdant place. But it is not at all what colonial residents would have experienced. In the last few decades there has been a movement to "redesign" these colonial revival gardens using our present-day knowledge of eighteenth-century gardens. Oftentimes in gardens this is done zealously and the historical colonial revival style is sacrificed in the name of something ostensibly more "historic." Yet Williamsburg has ingeniously steered a path through this minefield. In certain areas they have made an effort to re-create the eighteenth-century landscape, based on archeological research, while in other areas—where the colonial revival is at its most stunning—they have left well enough alone. This has the dual effect of making Williamsburg a continually enthralling aesthetic experience and also a more complexly interesting historical landscape as well.

    The centerpiece of the garden experience is the *Palace Gardens* arranged around the Georgian manor that was built by the Queen's emissary to the tobacco colony. Off to one side of the Governor's Palace lie a series of terraces that step down to one of the ravines that originally cut into the heart of town. Here gardeners maintained a large vegetable garden that once ran the length of the property along the terrace but which now only runs a third of the way. Like the citizens, the governor would have subsisted largely on produce and meats purchased at the market. But because he was required to host foreign dignitaries and visitors to the colony the garden was planted with specialty plants that could be used to supplement and enrich the table. One such plant was cardoon, a member of the globe locust family that could be used in soups to give them a rich taste. Signs that this was no ordinary vegetable garden are evident in the espaliered pears and apricots along the wall. Adjacent to the vegetable garden lies a formal parterre garden designed by Shurcliff as four quincunxes, two of which revolve around a circular center, the other two around ovals. The quincunx pattern, and particularly the alternating geometrical centers, are derived from a French tradition. In re-creating Williamsburg Shurcliff and his colleagues conducted extensive research of town records. While the original plans for the layout

OPPOSITE: *Victorian boxwood gardens adorn the Powell House.*

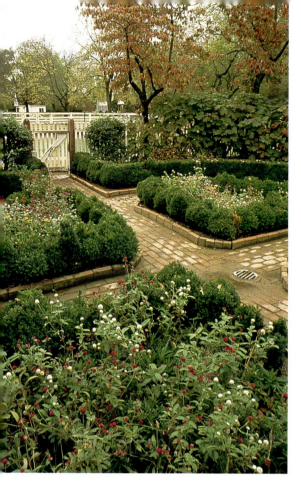

of streets showed the composition of lots, placement of fences, and even the location of certain trees, gardens were not included. However at nearby New Bern, North Carolina, a survey conducted by the French government at the same time that Williamsburg was being rebuilt showed that formal gardens very much in the French style were common among the town's wealthy citizens. The parterre garden was replanted about five years ago after a virulent winter storm destroyed much of the original boxwood. Crepe myrtle that anchored the outer beds also suffered and was replaced with holly that is not being trained into globes. From the far edge of the garden an aerial hedge of lindens (replacing live oaks, a strange selection given that tree's horizontal growing habit) enclosed a quiet lawn. Originally Shurcliff had planned to create another parterre garden here, but during construction gardeners discovered the skeletons of a hundred and fifty Civil War soldiers (identified by pewter buttons bearing the ensignia of Connecticut, Maine, and other northern regiments) and two women (presumably nurses). The bones were replaced, the area enclosed by hedge and roped off, and a plaque erected to commemorate the dead and indicate that the town has had other histories beside the colonial one celebrated.

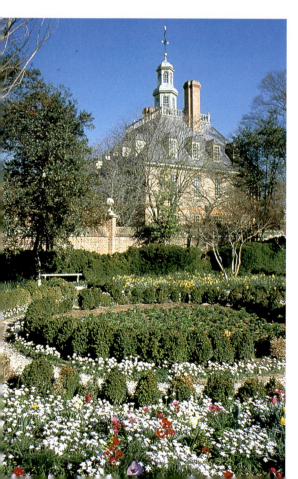

There are several other houses within the museum that feature gardens. Near the Governor's Palace is Wythe House, the residence of the one of the first law professors in the country who tutored Thomas Jefferson and other students at the college in the back room of his house. From here young Jefferson could have looked out upon his mentor's formal English-style garden, the grandeur of which must have appealed to this student's European tastes. The garden lies on axis with the back door and extends in a narrow line through the center of the property. A thick hedge of yew, defined by architectural "posts," frames each side of a meticulously trimmed lawn. Two borders of mixed annuals that illustrate a colonial disregard for "hot" or "cold" colors anchor the walls of the garden, accentuating its length and infusing the atmosphere with life. A brick path cuts through the center of the garden, ending in a wooden arbor, lying on a cross axis and covered with Carolina hornbeam, a delicate deciduous plant whose strange trunk has given it the common name "ironwood." Although it consumes an entire third of the property, Wythe's vegetable garden is too small to have supported the household entirely. Instead residents of Williamsburg, in contrast to their fellow Virginians living on rural plantations, benefited from a regular market in town.

Across the street from the Wythe property lies the Elkanah Deane house. Deane was a carriage maker who enjoyed a brisk business in mercantile Williamsburg, enough so to purchase a significant piece of property only a few doors from the Governor's Palace. However Deane could not have afforded the human workforce needed to maintain an opulent garden. He most likely spent the entire day toiling in his shop at the far end of the lot while his wife, even with the assistance of a few slaves, would have had her hands full with the household duties and a vegetable garden. Nonetheless, perhaps based on erroneous information about the sale price of the house in the eighteenth century, Shurcliff designed a French-inspired parterre garden that stretches the length of the property from the house to workshop. The garden is arranged in a system of three quincunxes, each with a geometrically different central bed. Originally the corners of the quincunxes were planted with gumball trees. But these were replaced with less messy lindens in the 1940s. At that time the garden was sunny, and the boxwood thrived, giving the intricate design a bold, vivid aspect. The beds were planted with an extravagant use of perennials.

Today the lindens are enormous and the parterres are in sorry shape. With the exception of a spring display of foxglove, phlox, and other flowers along the interior edge, the garden is essentially colorless. A debate is underway about its future. Archeologists are doubtful whether they could unearth any information about the original Deane garden due to the fact that two other houses have been erected and dismantled on the site since the eighteenth century. A strong voice has been raised in favor of removing the venerable lindens and restoring Shurcliff's lavish garden. Most probably a compromise will be reached in which the present garden will be removed, an excavation will be undertaken, and if no compelling information about the Deane garden is unearthed, the space will be replanted as a restoration of the Shurcliff design. Until then the quiet garden provides a cool respite during a museum visit.

OPPOSITE, TOP: *A classic southern touch—brick pathways, graceful plantings—are the pleasure ground for the Taliaferro-Cole house.*

OPPOSITE, BOTTOM: *The Palace Gardens are the centerpiece of Colonial Williamsburg.*

One of Carter's Grove's beautiful gardens

The James Getty house is an attempt to show the lifestyle of the middle class during the period. The house sits on the front portion of the property, bordering a courtyard in the rear that is surrounded by outbuildings—a separate kitchen, curing room, and so forth. Beyond this lays a vegetable and herb garden intermingled with choice ornamentals. The last third of the property was devoted to either an orchard or a paddock where a horse might rest after use, before being put out to pasture. Getty's vegetable garden is typical of the 1920s restoration style: a cleanly bifurcated plot with a grass path leading between two sets of square beds set off by black locust logs. The planting plan represents a colonial revival sensibility with plenty of color. Most obviously out of step with Getty's actual garden is the lawn that frames the beds. In colonial time grass lawns were only found in two places: in the common property located beyond the residential fence where they could be trimmed by a small army of sheep, pigs, and goats; and in the gardens of the wealthy who could afford to employ several gardeners to trim them by hand with a long scythe and then flatten them out with rolling stones.

The museum gardens continue to evolve. The current landscape curator says that they were shaken out of their complacency in the early 1990s as competition with other themed museums, like Disney World, became a real issue. The landscape has become a way to respond, and much care has been lavished to not only spruce the place up but to lead garden tours and educate people about colonial gardens. A new garden center, set up on Duke of Gloucester Street, runs programs throughout the summer.

At the far edge of town, Carter's Grove takes advantage of the outlying landscape.

VIRGINIA

15 Norfolk: Norfolk Botanical Gardens

LOCATION: EXIT 279 ON INTERSTATE 64, ADJACENT TO THE AIRPORT, FIVE MILES EAST OF DOWNTOWN NORFOLK

Local lore has it that when Thomas Thompson arrived in Norfolk from Austria in the 1930s he took one look at the maze of saltwater creeks and estuaries that cut through the area and envisioned that one day the city would rival Venice. That never happened and unfortunately, outside of the historic city center, Norfolk and Virginia Beach are a sprawling, jerimandered suburb of roads. The one exception is the Norfolk Botanical Gardens, begun in 1938 under the impetus of Thompson. During the Depression the Works Progress Administration employed so many workers that the original gardens, which encompassed 25 acres and were planted with over 4,000 azaleas, were built by an army of 200 women, most of whom were black. The gardens had grown to 250 acres by 1971, when 75 were sold to the local airport. The azaleas are still miraculous, and because the species selection is diverse their blooming cycle runs through the entire spring. The garden is also internationally recognized for its collections of camellias and rhododendrons, both of which were begun in the 1930s and have continued to be augmented over the years. In the 1960s one of the country's first sensory gardens for the blind was constructed here. Called the *Fragrance Garden*, it features witchhazel, roses, calycanthus, heliotrope, and entire array of old and modern flowers with both olfactory and textural characteristics. Formal gardens include a perennial plaza anchored by a large fountain and canal, an old sunken garden with the unusual juxtaposition of a fish pond and succulents, and *the Renaissance Court* and *Statuary Vista*, an allée of oaks and camellias built in the 1960s to provide Virginians with a taste of Versailles. To a greater and lesser degree, these formal gardens succeed, but the main attraction, as Thompson understood, is the natural beauty of the mature forest complemented by abundant azaleas and lazy Lake Whitehurst that encloses the gardens on three sides. As the state botanical garden there are concerts and events throughout the summer.

GARDEN OPEN: 9 am to 7 pm daily, April 15–October 15; 9 am to 5 pm daily, October 16–April 14. ADMISSION: $4 adults, $3 seniors, $2 children (6–18 years).

FURTHER INFORMATION FROM: 6700 Azalea Garden Road, Norfolk 23518
(757) 441-5830
www.communitylink.org/nbg

NEARBY SITES OF INTEREST: Hampton Roads Naval Museum, Virginia Marine Science Museum

Water is a central theme at the Norfolk Botanical Gardens.

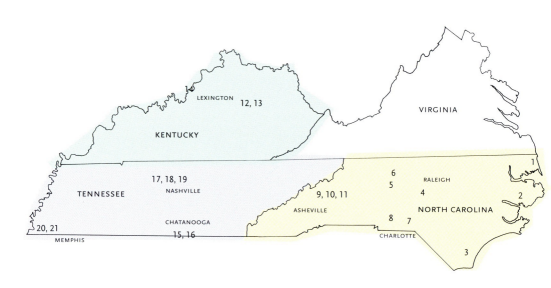

1 Roanoke Island: Elizabethan Gardens	8 Belmont: Daniel Stowe Botanical Garden	15 Chattanooga: Tennessee River Garden
2 New Bern: Tryon Place	9 Asheville: Biltmore Estate	16 Chattanooga: Reflection Riding
3 Wilmington: Arlie Gardens	10 Asheville: Botanical Gardens	17 Nashville: Cheekwood
4 Raleigh: J.C. Raulston Arboretum	11 Asheville: North Carolina Arboretum	18 Nashville: Hermitage
5 Chapel Hill: North Carolina Botanical Garden	12 Lexington: Ashland	19 Nashville: Scarritt-Bennett Center
6 Durham: Sarah P. Duke Gardens	13 Lexington: Lexington Cemetery	20 Memphis Dixon Gallery and Gardens
7 Charlotte: Wing Haven Gardens	14 Louisville: Cave Hill Cemetery	21 Memphis: Memphis Botanic Garden

TOBACCO COUNTRY

North Carolina, Kentucky, Tennessee

Stepping across the Virginia border into North Carolina we also step forward a hundred years to the height of what's called the country place era, that time at the end of the nineteenth and beginning of the twentieth centuries when American millionaires began building extravagant palaces outside the city. Fashionable Newport mansions were was born during this period, and so was the Biltmore Estate in Asheville, the enormous southern residence of George Vanderbilt. Some would argue that it is really a northern expression plunked down in the southern mountains. Indeed, as it was created by three prominent northerners (besides Vanderbilt, landscape architect Frederick Law Olmsted and architect Richard Morris Hunt) this might be the case. But it is also a generally American place, a symbol of New World ascendancy at the dawn of the twentieth century as well as a symbol of its excessive pride and wealth. Biltmore's landscape is considered one of Olmsted's finer works, and although all sorts of English tricks are used in the parklike grounds, the landscape architect masterfully undertook to orient the design toward the local context.

The local context has been fully embraced by the North Carolina Arboretum, a relatively new garden that interprets the regional landscape in a variety of interesting ways. Unlike most arboretums, ornamental flower gardens comprise a significant part of the collection, including the Quilt Garden where Appalachian traditions in quilt-making are implemented in flowers. Moving down from the mountains, toward

OPPOSITE: *The Wildflower Garden in Nashville*

TOBACCO COUNTRY

the coast, we stop for a moment at the Sarah P. Duke Gardens on the campus of Duke University. The historic Terrace Garden here was designed by Ellen Biddle Shipman, one of the most important American garden designers of the twentieth century, and it has been lovingly maintained over the years. At the ocean's edge we find two wonderful timepieces. The elegant restoration of Tryon Palace evokes the frontier glamour of the Queen's emissary to North Carolina just prior to the Revolution, and at the Elizabethan Gardens on Roanoke Island, an inspired formal garden provides a backdrop to the drama of the Lost Colony.

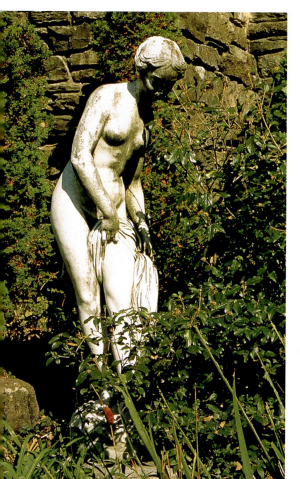

The grotto at Cheekwood in Nashville

And finally, the majestic rolling landscapes of Kentucky and Tennessee, represented here by some of the most beautiful, if quietest, landscape gardens anywhere. In Kentucky we include Cave Hill, one of the oldest landscape spaces in the country and a garden of incomparable beauty. In Tennessee there is John Chambliss' amateur masterwork Reflection Riding, a perfectly conceived landscape garden in the hills of Chattanooga.

TOBACCO COUNTRY: NORTH CAROLINA

Roanoke Island: Elizabethan Gardens

LOCATION: STATE ROUTE 345, OUTER BANKS, SOUTH OF KITTY HAWK, NEAR OREGON INLET

This is may arguably be the most haunted place in American history. Sir Walter Raleigh's "lost colony" made camp in the tangled woods that line this shallow coast in 1584, only to disappear three years later. Not a trace was found. In recent times a kind of homage has been created at the Elizabethan Gardens, which provides perhaps the most authentic glimpse back at the world the colonists left, and the Lost Colony theater, which re-imagines their fate. The gardens were designed and built by Innocenti and Webel, landscape architects who designed several important estates in the Northeast; construction was begun on the same day in 1953 that Elizabeth II was crowned. Innocenti and Webel understood very well the tightly prescribed aesthetics of the sixteenth-century English garden and employed them here to perhaps their best expression on these shores. The *Sunken Garden*, in the middle of the site, embodies the program. It is a perfectly square garden of low-lying, meticulously cut boxwood parterres filled to the brim with an ever-changing display of color. Of particular interest are the early summer months when the crepe myrtle that anchor the corners of the parterre explode in pink. Outside of the hedged confines of the *Sunken Garden*, the landscape serves up several other gardenesque experiences of a more and less historical English character, although the specific era diverges from the Elizabethan ever so slightly. There is a picturesque overlook near Albermarle Sound, a woodland garden, a grove of old live oaks, a formal rose garden, and several works of statuary and architecture, including the gate house that was inspired by a sixteenth-century orangerie and furnished with period works. The garden is lovingly maintained and well visited (the two seem to go together) as the summer months see the Outer Banks overwhelmed with tourists.

GARDEN OPEN: 9 am to 8 pm daily, June–Labor Day; 9 am to 5 pm daily, Labor Day–June. ADMISSION: $4.00 adults, $3.50 seniors, $1.00 youth.

FURTHER INFORMATION FROM: P.O. Box 1150, Manteo 27954
(252) 473-3234
www.outerbanks-nc.com/elizabethangardens

NEARBY SIGHTS OF INTEREST: Kitty Hawk, Cape Hatteras Lighthouse, Lost Colony

Traditional eighteenth-century organization divides the Elizabethan gardens into distinct rooms.

TOBACCO COUNTRY: NORTH CAROLINA

2 New Bern: Tryon Palace

LOCATION: OFF INTERSTATE 70, JUST EAST OF TOWN

GARDEN OPEN: 9 am to 5 pm Monday–Saturday, 1 pm to 5 pm Sunday, Labor Day–Memorial Day; open until 7 pm, Memorial Day–Labor Day. **ADMISSION:** $12 adults, $6 students.

FURTHER INFORMATION FROM: P.O. Box 1007, New Bern 28563
(800) 767-1580
tryonpalace.org

NEARBY SIGHTS OF INTEREST: New Bern National Cemetery

Tryon Palace was constructed by colonial Governor William Tryon in the early 1770s. But after only a short period as the residence of the king's proxy in North Carolina, Tryon saw his subjects revolt. For many years the Georgian manor served as a gathering place for the state legislature. In the 1940s as the palace was being restored, an eighteenth-century garden was planted. It is laid out as the fleur-de-lis pattern of boxwood filled with color-themed flowers and a central fountain. The pathwork of red brick unites the garden with North Carolina, while everything else seems to long for the old world. In addition to this focal point, there is a small walled kitchen garden of heirloom fruits and vegetables. It consists of varieties brought over from Europe, such as cardoon (*Cynara cardunculus*), a kind of artichoke, and plants found here on American shores, such as the runner bean. We find a more contemporary twist in the wilderness walk where native plants are featured. There is also a new garden of antique perennials, tastefully designed with herringbone brick paving and several wooden arbors.

The colonial ambassador's palace traditionally displayed French-influenced parterre gardens.

TOBACCO COUNTRY: NORTH CAROLINA

3 Wilmington: Arlie Gardens

LOCATION: OFF U.S. ROUTE 76, THREE MILES EAST OF WILMINGTON

GARDEN OPEN: 9 am to 5 pm Friday and Saturday, 1 pm to 5 pm Sunday, year-round.
ADMISSION: $8.

FURTHER INFORMATION FROM:
6206 Oleander Drive,
Wilmington 28403
www.arliegardens.
wilmington.org
(910) 791-5575

NEARBY SIGHTS OF INTEREST:
USS North Carolina Monument

The Arlie Gardens were originally designed 1891 as a social club for Pembroke Jones and his friends in Wilmington. The former landscape architect for Kaiser Wilhelm, R. A. Topel, was hired in the early years of this century to spruce things up a bit, and with Pembroke's wife, Sadie, he transformed the lodge into a wonderful landscape garden filled with statuary and native azaleas. The azaleas, which are knitted into the woods, are still the main attraction, and come to full bloom in April. During the winter low-blooming camellias transform the garden into a sea of color. The mature woods, which have been battered by a succession of hurricanes in recent years, are a true southern blend of stately magnolias and crooked live oaks. The spirit of the garden lies in its careful layout, with old brick walking paths manipulating the visitor's experience in ingenious ways. The sculptural pieces covered in moss or enclosed within a copse of dark trees, exude a feeling of mystery. At key points vistas of small ponds or a wide cavern of overarching live oaks suddenly come into view. Part of the ambience is due to the fact that the gardens have only been open to the public for a short time and thus are still largely unrestored. Although eventually this process will be welcomed, until then the gardens retain a bit of old world flavor with all its time-worn, burnished power.

4 Raleigh: J.C. Raulston Arboretum

LOCATION: EXIT 2 ON INTERSTATE 440

GARDEN OPEN: Dawn to dusk daily. ADMISSION: free.

FURTHER INFORMATION FROM:
North Carolina State University, Raleigh
(919) 515-3132

NEARBY SIGHTS OF INTEREST:
State Fairgrounds

Typically in order to have a garden in your name, you must donate a lot of money or land. But what happens when the donation is your soul, your life's work? This is the case with North Carolina State College Arboretum, which was carved out of nothing beginning in 1976 by professor of horticulture J. C. Raulston. When he died in a car accident in 1996, the college renamed the garden to honor his memory. The fundamental structure of the garden is composed of shrub and woody plants propagated in the last twenty years. Of these the arboretum boasts the largest collection of redbud, mondo grass, juniper, and nandina in the country. Near the central facilities in the middle of the complex are several large garden areas, including a terraced garden of predominantly white or light colored flowering plants. The design is based upon Sissinghurst in England. A display garden, a zen garden, and a perennial garden are also included. One favorite is the *Paradise Garden*, designed around a water feature with a bamboo dome. It is

The "tender perennials" modeled after traditional Persian gardens, in that all five senses are represented: there are edible, textural, visual, and smelly plants and, of course, the babbling brook. The *Japanese Garden* was designed as a traditional strolling garden with an exceptional collection of ornamental shrubs. The tree and woody plant collections are nationally recognized and describe the local landscape context.

GARDEN OPEN: 8 am to 5 pm Monday–Friday, year-round; 9 am to 6 pm Saturday, 1 pm to 6 pm Sunday, March–October; 10 am to 5 pm Saturday, 1 pm to 5 pm Sunday, November–March. **ADMISSION:** free.

FURTHER INFORMATION FROM: CB 3375, Totten Center, Chapel Hill 27599
(919) 962-0522

NEARBY SIGHTS OF INTEREST: University of North Carolina

5 Chapel Hill: North Carolina Botanical Garden

LOCATION: EXIT 273 ON INTERSTATE 40, ONTO STATE ROUTE 54 WEST, TO FINLEY GOLF COURSE ROAD

This is a young garden, in terms of organization, having been brought together only in the 1970s. But that fact overlooks several others—that parts of the various arboreta on-site have been under cultivation for almost one hundred years. The heart of the garden is its native plant and ecological garden areas, and these take the form of landscape exhibits. For instance, two trails wind through the gardens. One takes visitors into an upland preserve of oak–hickory association, while the other dips down into wetter areas. Throughout, the woods have been carefully edited and managed over time with an eye toward biodiversity. Of this you will witness a profusion of wildflowers such as trillium in the spring. A special border of wildflowers is utilized along the roadside, an area of tense interaction between people and nature that is softened by this simplest of interventions. The wetland garden is a coastal habitat that imitates what normally is found to the east of here, in more coastal areas. Rolling sand hills are an artifice used to structure the system. Of particular note is the pine savannah maintained by regular burning. In the upland area there is a mountain habitat of pines, tulip poplars, and such hardy flowering shrubs as azaleas and broadleaf rhododendrons that are typical of areas in the western part of the state. There is also a small display of ferns and shady plants that surround a rustic cabin, once used by the playwright Paul Green. A main attraction is the educational herb garden that presents a full array of culinary, medicinal, and industrial herbs (those used to make things). In addition to these areas, there are other natural areas that comprise the botanical gardens at large, but which are considered separate for various reasons. One of these is the Coker Arboretum, named for a professor of botany. It is a small, comfortable woody area with pleasant garden paths and a collection of exotic flowering plants set within the existing bones of a woodland. It has a much different historic and aesthetic sense than the rest of the garden, and has for years been a beloved destination on campus.

Informal, folksy aesthetics ground the North Carolina Botanical Garden.

6 Durham: Sarah P. Duke Gardens

GARDEN OPEN: 8 am to dusk daily, year-round. **ADMISSION:** free.

FURTHER INFORMATION FROM: Duke University, Box 90341, Durham 27708
(919) 684-3698

NEARBY SIGHTS OF INTEREST: Duke Homestead

LOCATION: ANDERSEN STREET, JUST OFF DURHAM FREEWAY (STATE ROUTE 147) ON THE DUKE UNIVERSITY CAMPUS

When Duke University was founded in the early part of the twentieth century the old ravine on the edge was always intended to be a lake. But economics and big plans being what they are, the ravine was filled with garbage rather than water, and not much happened for many years. In the 1930s a medical professor who lived near the pit and walked past the debris each day on his way to work began agitating for a garden to be built there. He persuaded benefactor Sarah P. Duke to put up the funds, and a small garden was planted. Of course, this being a ravine, and with the next big rain the whole affair was washed down the drain so to speak. By now the quest for the garden was in the hands of Duke's daughter, Mary Duke Biddle, and she used her Philadelphia connections to bring down the landscape architect Ellen Biddle Shipman to see if she could fix things. Shipman created a system of sturdy stone retaining walls and terraces imbued with the sense of Italy but structured to train views inward across the natural topography of the site. The terraces fan out in response to the natural lay of the land, and are defined by large magnolias on each side and two stone garden structures, one of which has been converted into a gift shop. At the top of the terraces rests a large pergola covered with an immense lump of wisteria. It is an iconographic image, employed in most of the garden's marketing materials, that greets visitors when they first enter. At the bottom of the terrace, Shipman designed an irregularly shaped fish pond engulfed in perennials and defined by boxwood. Behind the terrace the designer also executed a grottolike rock garden in New Jersey limestone. The stone is turned on its end and struck into the ground like a sword, creating the illusion, derived from Asiatic traditions, of a larger landscape (mountains). The area just beyond the rock garden is a wonderful large bowl of grass where students often sunbathe, surrounded by a thin scrim of woods that conveniently cuts this place off from the rest of the world. Beyond the terraces the garden reverts to a naturalistic setting. The *H. L. Blomquist Garden of Native Plants* occupies a large corner. Named after the founder of the university's botany department, this garden contains over 900 varieties of wildflowers culled from the entire southeast region. There are so many interesting examples of the native landscape laid out in such an exciting array that visitors often take to the peaceful little gazebo in the center of the maze of winding paths just to gain perspective. The latest addition to the garden collections is a complexly layered *Asiatic Arboretum*. This is a curious amalgam of a nineteenth century arboretum (many specialized in hardy species from Asia) and a traditional tea garden. This latter character is achieved largely through the use of architectural components such as bridges, while the design is more reminiscent of such nineteenth-century landscapes as the Arnold Arboretum in Boston. Because of the importance of the Shipman garden—her only public commission still in existence—the Duke Garden houses a research institution that frequently hosts symposia and lecturers, always attracting those interested in historic gardens who venture here as a kind of pilgrimage.

Italian Terrace at the Sarah P. Duke Gardens, designed by Ellen Biddle Shipman

GARDEN OPEN: 3 pm to 5 pm Tuesday and Wednesday, 2 pm to 5 pm Sunday, year-round. **ADMISSION:** free.

FURTHER INFORMATION FROM:
248 Ridgewood Avenue,
Charlotte 28209
(704) 331-0664

NEARBY SIGHTS OF INTEREST:
Charlotte Nature Museum

7 Charlotte: Wing Haven Gardens & Bird Sanctuary

LOCATION: WOODLAWN (EXIT 6 ON I-77) TO PARK ROAD, TO HILLSIDE, TO WESTFIELD, THREE MILES FROM DOWNTOWN

Wing Haven got its start in the suburban backyard of Elizabeth and Edwin Clarkson in the 1920s when they took in a little bird whose mother had been killed by a hawk. The lot at the time was virtually treeless and lifeless, with the ground a hard-packed red clay. Over a sixty-year period Elizabeth transformed the property into an amazingly lush garden home for "tommy," the bluebird they had rescued, and eventually hundreds of his friends. A formal grass terrace occupies the heart of this aviary garden, ringed about with a thin brick edge and pillows of white flowers. A few sculptural pieces sit around the edge, which quickly dissipates into a wooded area that denies that this was ever a wasteland. The plant selection was done with a careful eye toward attracting birds, so we find plenty of seed- and fruit-bearing trees, and also shrubs considered conducive to nesting. There are even several birdbaths around the gardens, which actually provide a source of drinking water more than a place for bathing.

A formal grass terrace forms the heart of this aviary garden.

8 Belmont: Daniel Stowe Botanical Garden

LOCATION: FROM CHARLOTTE ON INTERSTATE 85, TAKE EXIT 26, MAIN STREET SOUTH FOR FIVE MILES THROUGH BELMONT, LEFT ON NEW HOPE ROAD

GARDEN OPEN: 9 am to 6 pm daily; closes at 5 pm during the winter. ADMISSION: free.

FURTHER INFORMATION FROM:
6500 New Hope Road,
Belmont 28012
(704) 825-4490
www.stowegarden.org

NEARBY SIGHTS OF INTEREST:
Carowinds, Charlotte Nature Museum

The Daniel Stowe Botanical Garden is an ambitious effort that indicates this city's deep enthusiasm for gardening. The property and a considerable endowment were donated by textile magnate Daniel Stowe and his wife Alene. It features rolling Piedmont woodlands focused upon a lake. The first ten acres were developed in 1991 with a large perennial garden as the main attraction. The style is contemporary, meaning that you will see a tapestry of color arranged in soft lines and contrasting texture, much in the vein of Roberto Burle-Marx. It is distinguished by four areas: the *Allée Garden*, aptly named for its chute of evergreens; the *Scroll Garden* where any specific color palette is abandoned for rolling sweeps of "airy plants," such as the rain lilies found at the center; and the *Ribbon and Serpentine Gardens*, both displaying a wild array of hot and warm colors respectively. Just beyond the visitors pavilion is a collection of shrubs and small colorful trees comprising the Four Seasons Garden, so named for its continual color throughout the year. The onsite *Cottage Garden* is overly large, and hence probably not appropriate for the name; however the abundant collection of hollyhocks, phlox, narcissus, and other old-fashioned flowers have the power to transport us back to earlier parts of the twentieth century. The last established garden is the *Canal Garden* where tropicals surround a plaza and reflecting pool, punctuated along its length by "dancing fountains."

A structured canal acts as a spine for a new collection.

TOBACCO COUNTRY: NORTH CAROLINA

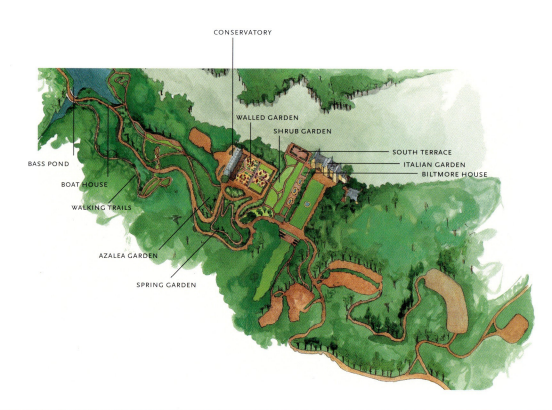

9 Asheville: Biltmore Estate

LOCATION: EXIT 50 ON INTERSTATE 40, FOLLOW SIGNS

GARDEN OPEN: 9 am to 5 pm daily, year-round, except major holidays. ADMISSION: $29.95 adults, $22.50 children over 5 years.

FURTHER INFORMATION FROM: 1 North Pack Square, Asheville 28801
(800) 543-2961
www.biltmore.com

NEARBY SIGHTS OF INTEREST: Carl Sandburg Home, Pisgah National Forest, Folk Art Center

In 1895 the Biltmore Estate described itself as the most ambitious home ever conceived in America. Even in such an excessive age as ours the towering French chateau-inspired mansion still creates a feeling of awe and bewilderment. Nothing in Newport dares compete. It stands, as it always has, without peer.

Biltmore was conceived by three extraordinary men. First was George Vanderbilt, the son of William Henry Vanderbilt and grandson of paterfamilias and railroad tycoon Cornelius. Vanderbilt fell in love with the landscape of the North Carolina mountains when on a trip there with his mother in 1888, and fashioned in his mind a palatial rural estate. Much of his inspiration was drawn from Shelburne Farms, the gentleman's farm on the shore of Lake Champlain in Vermont that his sister Lila had built with her husband William Seward Webb. The Shelburne landscape was designed by Frederick Law Olmsted, the most famous landscape architect in America at that time, best known for creating Central Park in Manhattan (1857) and Prospect Park in Brooklyn (1871). It was fortuitous for Vanderbilt that Olmsted's relations with Webb were souring as the century neared its end, and he snapped up the designer to come make his fortune in the Great Smokey Mountains. Richard Morris Hunt, the society architect of opulent summer cottages in Newport, Rhode Island, completed the team. He countered Olmsted's countrified ruralism with a strong sense of European classicism. What arose from their work, appears, at its wors, as a dialogue between contrasting aesthetics. At its best it is a supreme example of how architecture inevitably derives most of its strength from landscape.

The gardens surrounding the oversized chateau (there are 250 rooms, four acres of floor area, and a priceless collection of furniture and textiles) began as experiments in carefully calculated European formality, and eventually give over into rolling, park-like naturalistic areas. Surprisingly Olmsted was deft at both, although we most commonly associate the English romantic park aesthetic with him. *The Terrace Garden* lies adjacent to the house. The Italianate Renaissance design of this space features sculpted pools in the horizontal plane that are cradled by meticulously trimmed lawn. The architecture of the house is extended out in the form of an ornate balustrade to make the garden seem like an "outdoor room," thus appropriate for spillover from important gatherings inside the spacious ball rooms. The great showiness of Biltmore is omnipotent in the *Walled Garden* located below the house. Olmsted originally intended this handsomely enclosed space as an English kitchen garden, but Vanderbilt desired a purely ornamental approach.

OPPOSITE: *The conservatory and Walled Garden in summer*

TOP: *The Walled Garden*

MIDDLE: *Spring Garden*

BOTTOM: *The rose garden*

The planting design evolves through the seasons in a constant show of floral color—thousands of bulbs in the spring, annuals in the summer, and mums in the fall. The lower half of the garden houses the rose collection, featuring a couple thousand plants, from modern tea hybrids to an impressive gathering of heirloom varieties. Many of these were actually cultivated specifically for the Vanderbilts.

Presiding over the gardens is the majestic *Conservatory*, designed by Hunt in a similarly French vein. Olmsted also played a role in the siting of the building, urging Hunt to sink it slightly below grade so that the impressive vistas from the mansion (which many consider the soul of the Biltmore) would be preserved. A $2.5 million dollar restoration has just wrapped up and now the building is open to the public. The central chamber of the Conservatory contains an assortment of palms. The east side of the house is considered the cool side, and features azaleas, camellias, and bulbs, while the west, the hot side, shelters begonias and fuschias. The structure is still used as the working horticultural center for the entire estate.

Connecting these formal gardens to the rest of the estate is the *Ramble*, a small arboretum of ornamental trees and shrubs designed around a meandering path. It is a famous Olmstedian gesture, showing up vividly in his design for Central Park. Here it makes its appearance in a mountainous context, capitalizing on the romantic vistas of the surrounding landscape. From the *Ramble* guests were encouraged to explore the rest of the estate, which Olmsted designed as a managed wildlands. The forest is still an example of some of the best management practices in the country, with a healthy succession of plant materials, preserved viewscapes, and plenty of wildlife (most especially deer). Notable features include the *Esplanade*, a turf allée that climbs up the hill toward the mansion and is defined by a complex of ornate ramps called the *Rampe Douce*. Perhaps the singularly most

sublime feature of the entire estate is the entrance drive where Olmsted manipulated the carriage (or car) rider's experience of the landscape to almost perfection.

The Biltmore was restored and preserved in the 1960s and 1970s by William Cecil, grandson of George Vanderbilt. The dairy farm that once adorned the property was converted into a winery and a new inn is opening for the 2000 season, further extending the magical world of the Vanderbilts to the wider public. As has always been the case visitors are encouraged to spend much of their time outdoors, imbibing the natural religion of the place that once so captivated its progenitor.

ABOVE: *Tulips abloom in Biltmore's Walled Garden*

BELOW: *Grand architectural elements imbue the landscape with French aesthetics.*

TOBACCO COUNTRY: NORTH CAROLINA

GARDEN OPEN: Dawn to dusk.
ADMISSION: free.

FURTHER INFORMATION FROM:
151 W. T. Weaver Boulevard,
Asheville 28804
(828) 252-5190

NEARBY SIGHTS OF INTEREST:
Biltmore Estate, Cradle of Forestry

10 Asheville: Botanical Gardens at Asheville

LOCATION: UNIVERSITY OF NORTH CAROLINA AT ASHEVILLE CAMPUS, ON W. T. WEAVER BOULEVARD

The gardens grew up with the campus at UNCA. About the time the small college evolved into the state institution it is today, a dedicated gardener, Mrs. Bruce Shinn, canvassed the community to develop a sizable garden there. The garden has always been focused upon native plants, and was designed in the 1960s by landscape architect Doan Ogden as an unfolding woodland landscape. The trail takes visitors from the parking lot, across rumbling Reed Creek, and up through a southern Appalachian deciduous forest. The layers have been carefully managed to create a thick, varied tapestry of plants, including a brilliant display of spring wildflowers on the ground plane. Along the trail there are numerous places to rest where views of the land have been choreographed to showcase the local flora. A 400-foot stone wall follows the trail, providing structure to the scene. At the far end of the walk lies a 100-foot arbor adorned with climbing vines and bulbs. Nearby, the woods opens up into a heath meadow that anchors views across to a full display of naturalized azaleas. The *Deer and Moss Trail* takes one past a small rock garden to the *Botany Center*. Built in the 1980s this structure houses information about the gardens, education programs, and a collection of insectivorous plants. The gardens are a mainstay in Asheville, and although completely volunteer run and donation driven, have thrived.

The deep woods resonate with subtle beauty at the Asheville Botanical Garden.

11 Asheville: North Carolina Arboretum

LOCATION: STATE ROUTE 191 TO BENT CREEK RANCH ROAD TO WESLEY BRANCH ROAD, SOUTHWEST OF DOWNTOWN ASHEVILLE

GARDEN OPEN: 8 am to 9 pm daily, year-round. ADMISSION: free.

FURTHER INFORMATION FROM:
100 Frederick Law Olmsted Way, Asheville 28806
(828) 665-2492
www.ncarboretum.org

NEARBY SIGHTS OF INTEREST:
Biltmore Estate

ABOVE: *The Quilt Garden at the North Carolina Arboretum*

One of Frederick Law Olmsted's intentions for George Vanderbilt's estate was the creation of an arboretum. While that vision was partly realized at Biltmore, it has finally been fleshed out at the state arboretum, organized in the early 1980s. It is run by the University of North Carolina and occupies an area of woodlands located at the conjunction of Pisgah National Forest and Bent Acre Experimental Forest. For the last ten years the existing canopy has been maintained with a keen eye toward plant conservation and amended with various idea gardens. The main feature, of course, is the stunning tree collection, much of which was planted eighty years ago. Upland hickory–oak association predominates, as do tulip poplars, mountain laurel, and various types of maple. A circuit of walking paths takes visitors through the cool forest, which is penetrated by mountain streams filled with fish. In the core garden area there are several intelligently presented idea gardens. The most popular is the *Quilt Garden*, a square of some twenty raised beds that in the height of the season are filled with colorful annuals and perennials to form a clearly delineated quilt pattern. The idea is Victorian, but the implementation is purely North Carolina and meant to invoke the Appalachian tradition of quilt making. Native plants have become a central focus of the arboretum, and the relatively young home demonstration garden that features plants taken from the surrounding forest and dressed-up for the suburban yard is a crowd pleaser. There is also a *Heritage Garden* filled with plants and herbs used in local crafts like basket-making and a *Stream Garden* where the course of a mountain stream, and its riparian environment, is created abstractly using stones and plant materials. The woods, however, draw most people. Throughout the seasons they evolve and change, and whether it is late fall when the symphony of color concludes or early spring when the world class woodland azalea collection comes into chorus, it is always as Olmsted envisioned: a dynamic landscape that evokes the natural beauty of the North Carolina mountains.

12 Lexington: Ashland

LOCATION: CORNER OF RICHMOND ROAD AND SYCAMORE ROAD, ON THE EAST SIDE OF TOWN

GARDEN OPEN: 10:00 am to 4:30 pm Monday–Saturday, 1:00 pm to 4:30 pm Sunday, year-round. Closed Mondays, November–March.

ADMISSION: $6 adults, $3 students, $2 children.

FURTHER INFORMATION FROM:
120 Sycamore Road,
Lexington 40502
(606) 266-8581

NEARBY SIGHTS OF INTEREST:
Mary Todd Lincoln Home

As an unsuccessful presidential candidate three times over, Henry Clay was heard to proclaim: "better right than president." Such conviction may seem foreign today, but for Clay—a heroic figure in Kentucky history—it was all part of his identity as a man of integrity. Clay adhered to the agrarian ideal that character was tied to the land, and like Jefferson and Washington a generation earlier, he built a magnificent working estate in his hometown of Lexington. Ashland, so named for the abundance of blue ash on the property, was formed by Clay over many years, during visits home from Washington, D.C. (where he served in Congress and then as secretary of state). The landscape encompasses a variety of typical English-style design attributes, to which Clay gave a unique homespun quality. The entrance drive proceeds through a handsome grove of cedars and catalpas, underplanted with a scrim of shrubs and naturalized bulbs, laid out in a graceful arch that keeps the house veiled from view until the last moment. The trick may be European but the plant vocabulary is completely Kentucky. The same is true for the rear areas, which feature a large lawn and a savannah pasture where livestock grazed on native bluegrass. Clay's house was dismantled in 1853 by his son and rebuilt on the same foundation, to the same plan, but with an updated flair of ornamenture. Clay and his heirs also enjoyed a formal garden on the grounds; however this has been lost to time. In 1951 the local garden club created a new "historic" garden just to the side of where the original lay. This garden is probably a lot fancier and more formal than Clay's. A long rectangle enclosure, the garden features six small parterres, each of which is classically trained on a central feature (usually a specimen tree) and perfectly balanced. The edge of the larger space is defined by a perennial border, lead planters, and clipped euonymus, culminating in iron gates at each end. The parterres use boxwood and brick to create an architectonic structure, over which colorful patterns of blooming groundcover create patterning. Several sculptural elements reside in the garden, including an Italian bronze statue of a boy with a birdcage. One parterre (number 6) is executed all in herbs and designed in a checkerboard pattern with a grid of figs to provide weight. The six parterres were designed by Henry Fletcher Kenney of Cincinnati, with one redesigned after storm damage by Innocenti and Webel of New York City. Set off into the woods is a small garden composed entirely of peonies, the gift of a generous donor.

The lush boxwood garden at Ashland connotes a deep mystery.

| TOBACCO COUNTRY: KENTUCKY

GARDEN OPEN: 8 am to 5 pm daily. **ADMISSION:** free.

FURTHER INFORMATION FROM:
833 West Main Street,
Lexington 40508
(606) 255-5522

NEARBY SIGHTS OF INTEREST:
Mary Todd Lincoln Home

13 Lexington: Lexington Cemetery

LOCATION: OFF MAIN STREET, NORTHWEST OF TOWN, NEAR THE BYPASS

The Lexington Cemetery was originally laid out in 1849 in response to a cholera epidemic. The tract was originally known as Boswell's Woods, thirty acres of forest that have steadily been increased to 170. Besides an incredible selection of stately canopy trees, the cemetery has become known for its flowering ornamentals and shrubs. The most exceptional tree in the landscape is an American linden dating to before the cemetery's organization, and now sitting next to the grave of Henry Clay. According to the record books, at 101 feet in height and 18.5 feet in circumference, it is the second largest linden of its kind in America.

Sensitive touches in this bald cypress, placed just inside the lake's edge at Lexington Cemetery

14 Louisville: Cave Hill Cemetery

LOCATION: GRINSTEAD DRIVE, OFF INTERSTATE 64, EAST OF DOWNTOWN

Cemeteries had their renaissance in the mid- to late-nineteenth century when American cities began to realize that it was more prudent to bury their dead outside of the town limits. As such, cemeteries began to take on a pastoral character—forerunners to the parks that would begin to be built after the Civil War. Mount Auburn, in Boston, was the first romantic park cemetery, and shortly to follow was Cave Hill. Designed and planted in 1848, Cave Hill is much more than an arboretum. It is a garden of majestic trees set within a rolling, picturesque landscape reminiscent of the great English manor estates. The tree collection features many notable specimens, including several beeches that predate the cemetery itself. American holly, cypress, yews, and several kinds of larches complete the scene. Underplanted beneath the large trees are various ornamental shrubs, including lots of azaleas that bloom in the middle of the spring. The fall comes alive as the foliage turns. While individual trees are in themselves beautiful, the most stunning feature of the garden is its overall romantic aspect. The winding drives that cut through the landscape there are artfully composed views of small lakes, rolling landscape, and tremendous

GARDEN OPEN: 8 am to 5 pm daily. **ADMISSION:** free.

FURTHER INFORMATION FROM:
701 Baxter Avenue,
Louisville 40204
(502) 451-5630

NEARBY SIGHTS OF INTEREST:
Belle of Louisville, Louisville Slugger

ABOVE: *The traditions of England are embodied in the history of Cave Hill.*

trees. Small cups or plazas are carved out around the grounds to provide destinations within the garden. These often include fountains such as Tingley Fountain, a hundred-year-old artifact that features a grouping of women with outstretched hands from whose fingers water flows. The gravestones also provide a sculptural counterpoint to the landscape, with many dating back to the nineteenth century. The most famous personage buried here is none other than fried chicken king Colonel Sanders.

GARDEN OPEN: 1 pm to 5 pm April–October. **ADMISSION:** $8 adults, $4 children.

FURTHER INFORMATION FROM:
22573 Highway 41,
Chattanooga 37419
(423) 756-8800

NEARBY SIGHTS OF INTEREST:
Hunter Art Museum,
Tennessee River Gorge

15 Chattanooga: Tennessee River Garden

LOCATION: WEST ON INTERSTATE 24 TO EXIT 174, 2.7 MILES

If beautiful places need beautiful gardens, then the Tennessee River Garden does its job. The landscape, situated with stunning views of the Tennessee River Gorge, provides an incredible structure for the garden, which after three years of cultivation is now abloom with abundant wildflowers. In the upland areas meadows contain a variety of naturalized species (meaning they were imported from Europe more than a hundred years ago), including ox-eye daisies and Queen Anne's lace. As the terrain dips into the limestone and sandstone crags that characterize this picturesque region an indigenous palette takes over. In all there are ten acres with stunning waterfalls and romantic views punctuating the experience.

16 Chattanooga: Reflection Riding

LOCATION: BROWNS FERRY ROAD EXIT ON INTERSTATE 24, CUMMINGS HIGHWAY, THEN FOLLOW SIGNS

GARDEN OPEN: Dawn to dusk daily, year-round. ADMISSION: $6 adults, $3 children.

FURTHER INFORMATION FROM: 400 Garden Road, Chattanooga 37416 (423) 821-9582 www.chattanooga.net/rriding/

NEARBY SIGHTS OF INTEREST: Chickamauga National Military Park

John Chambliss was one of those naturally intelligent beings whose simple integrity and honest curiosity had the fortuitous result of leading to great things. In this case one of these great things is a landscape garden of little compare. Reflection Riding began in the 1920s when Chambliss learned about a scheme proposed by Adolph Ochs, a prominent businessman and later owner of *the New York Times,* to build a hanging garden on the slopes of Lookout Mountain in Chattanooga. The plan fell through, but through a fluke deal Chambliss—not a wealthy man—acquired almost two hundred acres of land in the vicinity. He studied the great landscape texts of the nineteenth and twentieth centuries, including a biography of Charles Eliot and the classic landscape designs of Kimball and Hubbard, which articulated the basic idea that the landscape is essentially a work of art melded on a large scale to create visual and experiential effects. Chambliss took this concept to heart and over the next forty years, with the assistance of several prominent landscape architects, he fashioned his property into a series of vistas, rambles, and other classic landscape features. The palette is entirely native, and at the same time that Chambliss created artistic expressions he was also making an environmental statement. Today the garden is a clearinghouse for native plants in the region. As the name suggests, the landscape is organized according to the pace of a horse, and perhaps is best understood while riding through. It is also a reflective place—a word used to evoke both the spiritual aspect of the landscape and its unique quality of light. Horticulturist will enjoy the great diversity of plants, while design-minded visitors will swoon at the crafted meadows, roadways, and framed vistas.

ABOVE: *A traditional English "riding" transforms the Tennessee landscape*

OPPOSITE: *The Tennessee River Gorge provides a picturesque canvas for a scene of wildflowers.*

17 Nashville: Cheekwood

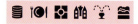

GARDEN OPEN: 9 am to 5 pm Monday–Saturday, 11 am to 5 pm Sunday, year-round except major holidays and the third Saturday in April; open until 8 pm Monday–Thursday, April 15–Labor Day. **ADMISSION:** $8 adults, $7 seniors, $5 children.

FURTHER INFORMATION FROM: 1200 Forrest Park Drive, Nashville 37205
(615) 356-8000
www.cheekwood.org

NEARBY SIGHTS OF INTEREST: Stone River National Battlefield

The Japanese garden takes advantage of the steep slope to create a layering of form and color.

LOCATION: FORREST PARK DRIVE, OFF PAGE ROAD AND BELLE MEADE DRIVE, ABOUT EIGHT MILES SOUTHWEST OF DOWNTOWN NASHVILLE

Cheekwood was the family estate of the Cheek family. The limestone Georgian style residence was constructed in the 1920s and now houses a recognized art collection, including American paintings from the 1930s as well as American decorative arts. The gardens were designed by Bryant Fleming in the 1920s, and reflect a strong European influence particularly in the terrace gardens that surround the house. These were originally very architectural in their composition, drawing on Italian inspiration. But over the years an attempt has been made to soften the aesthetic with the addition of colors. The *Boxwood Garden,* located near the house, is an intimate green space restored by Michael van Valkenburgh and given lively color by the addition of perennial beds and exotic shrubs. A pool occupies the center space, overlooked by a wisteria arbor and statues of Urania and Thalia. The *Color Garden* is the most stunning, visually, of all the gardens, particularly in the late spring when the avenue of crepe myrtle that leads to the space comes into bloom. Within the garden there are lush sweeps of flowers descending a sloped lawn. Archways carry a heavy abundance of roses, while a wall of ivy provides depth to what has over the years become a playfully rich field of rainbow color. A more naturalistic approach informs the design of the *Dogwood Garden,* so named for the plethora of these trees lining the path. Underpinning the brilliant specimen trees is a multilayered ground plane of hostas, astilbe, and hydrangeas arranged in an overflowing, patchwork manner.

18 Nashville: Hermitage, Home of Andrew Jackson

LOCATION: EXIT 221 ON INTERSTATE 40, FOUR MILES ALONG OLD HICKORY BOULEVARD

It is said that Old Hickory was a tough man. But when we walk into his gardens, Andrew Jackson seems to melt into sentimentality. The Hermitage was Jackson's sometime home when he was away from Washington, D. C., and the task of putting his unmistakable stamp on the affairs of the early nineteenth century. First Lady Rachel Jackson was a garden lover, and adjacent to the house she planted a formal garden derived from European traditions, with which she would have been thoroughly familiar. When she died unexpectedly in 1832 the garden became a kind of memorial. Yet Jackson and his heirs were unable to devote the time necessary to truly keep it up, and in 1889 it had to be completely restored. The structure of the garden is magical, with a pattern of stone-edged beds arranged in a radial manner and an allée of crepe myrtle connecting it with the house. The beds are planted in a rustic, informal manner, and filled with scrappy period varieties, such

GARDEN OPEN: 9 am to 5 pm daily, year-round. **ADMISSION:** $9.50 adults, $8.50 seniors, $4.50 children.

FURTHER INFORMATION FROM:
4580 Rachel's Lane,
Hermitage, Nashville 37076
(615) 889-9909
www.thehermitage.com

NEARBY SIGHTS OF INTEREST:
Grand Old Opry, Cragfont

Rachel Jackson loved gardens, and Andrew loved Rachel, as evidenced by this commemorative garden at The Hermitage.

TOBACCO COUNTRY: TENNESSEE

The gardens are a counterpoint to the neoclassical house.

as peonies, irises, and heirloom roses. The atmosphere is deeply romantic, longing to transport us to another time. Although we might not think of Jackson as domestic, this garden has become a kind of last symbol of his life—a symbol deeply connected to the love he shared with his wife. In the corner of the garden lies their common tomb gently enclosed by flowers

19 Nashville: Scarritt-Bennett Center

LOCATION: 18TH STREET, BETWEEN GRAND AVENUE AND EDGEHILL AVENUE

GARDEN OPEN: Dawn to dusk daily. ADMISSION: free.

FURTHER INFORMATION FROM:
1008 19th Avenue South,
Nashville 37212
(615) 340-7471
www.scarrittbennett.org

NEARBY SIGHTS OF INTEREST:
Country Music Hall of Fame, Belmont Mansion

The Scarritt-Bennett Center is a progressive theological seminary and conference center with a strong emphasis on cross-cultural and multidenominational dialogue. A major component of this focus concerns the environment, and that growing area of enviro-theology, which holds—among other things—that degradation of the earth by humans has spiritual connotations. Even unbelievers should stiffen at such a thought, and to make the point more strongly, the center created the *In Defense of Creation* organic and composting garden. The name of the garden comes from a well-known liturgical document composed by the United Methodist Council of Bishops that made certain points about the "wholeness" of the earth and the "wholeness" of humanity. The garden takes a proactive stand in this regard. A massive composting endeavor occupies its physical and philosophical center. Everything organic from the center as well as refuse from staff members' homes is brought to the garden and mixed with leaves, grass clippings, and soil. The process is daylighted for visitors to see what composting entails and learn to do it themselves. The natural fertilizer is then used in a pretty vegetable garden, which provides the center with all of its fresh foods—thus completing the regenerative cycle. The center is also surrounded by a pleasant arboretum and features a small perennial garden.

The In Defense of Creation organic garden at Scarritt-Bennett has a philosophical and social focus.

20 Memphis: Dixon Gallery and Gardens

LOCATION: I-240 TO GETWELL EXIT NORTH; RIGHT AT PARK AVENUE, EIGHT MILES EAST OF DOWNTOWN MEMPHIS.

GARDEN OPEN: 11 am to 5 pm Tuesday–Saturday, 1 pm to 5 pm Sunday, year-round except major holidays. **ADMISSION:** $5 adults, $4 seniors, $3 students.

FURTHER INFORMATION FROM:
4339 Park Avenue, Memphis 38117
(901)761-2409
www.dixon.org

NEARBY SIGHTS OF INTEREST:
Graceland

Margaret and Hugo Dixon began developing their city estate in Memphis in the 1940s by employing Mr. Dixon's sister, landscape architect Hope Crutchfield, to design the gardens. The Dixons and Crutchfield departed from the formal French grid and moved across the channel to England with the parklike setting of rolling lawn, framed vistas, and strolling paths that gently enclose a living gallery of outdoor statuary. Two indoor garden spaces were built over the years: a greenhouse devoted to fairly utilitarian endeavors and a camellia house protecting these subtropical beauties from the relatively harsh winters of Memphis. A major attraction for visitors is the cutting garden where curators gather vibrant flowers for the interior spaces. Although the plants are grown like a crop, this type of garden has a particular power—especially as a slight breeze brushes through the space and the full carpet of color sways. The formal gardens were conceived to display sculpture. Their rickety old brick paths exude an antique feel, complemented by bronze sculptures that wear the patina of age. A delicate selection of boxwood and other herbaceous plants—tending toward green—frame the space.

21 Memphis: Memphis Botanic Garden

LOCATION: IN AUDUBON PARK, CORNER OF PARK STREET AND CHERRY STREET

The Memphis Botanic Garden began life when local businessman E. H. Crump donated a part of his city estate to create Audubon Park in 1953. Soon after, a renegade iris society set up shop in one corner of the park. Several years and thousands of narcissi later, landscape architect George Madlinger came on the scene and helped formalize the *de facto* garden as a major urban horticultural center. Today nearly a hundred acres are planted with different theme and natural gardens, including a stunning landscape of rolling fields and mature trees. Madlinger began with a *Japanese Garden*, which was further built out in 1985 by master designer Koichi Kawana. The Japanese Garden is still the soul of the whole botanic garden. It has a very open, expansive character with a major amorphous lake at its center and such striking architectural features as the red bridge. In recent years, with the growing recognition among public gardens that they need educational components, the garden has developed a *Children's Garden*, with a significant butterfly habitat at its center. The *Rose Garden* is substantial and features all-America selections, while the daffodil hill, wildflower garden, and dogwood trail offer opportunities to experience the once verdant hilly topography of the area.

GARDEN OPEN: 9:00 am to 6:00 pm Monday–Saturday, 11:00 am to 6:00 pm Sunday, March–October; closes at 4:30 pm during the winter.
ADMISSION: $4 adults, $3 seniors and students, $2 children.

FURTHER INFORMATION FROM:
750 Cherry Road, Memphis 38117
(901) 685-1566

NEARBY SIGHTS OF INTEREST:
Graceland, Sun Studio

The modernist visitor center at the Memphis Botanic Garden.

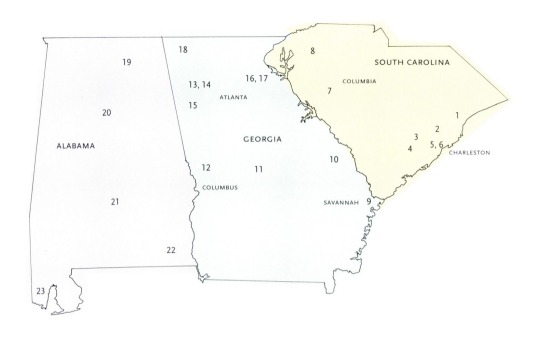

1 Murrells Inlet: Brookgreen Gardens
2 Moncks Corner: Cypress Gardens
3 Hartsville: Kalmia Gardens of Coker College
4 Pinesville: Middleton Place
5 Charleston: Magnolia Plantation
6 Charleston: Heyward-Washington House
7 Columbia: Riverbanks Botanical Garden
8 Clemson: South Carolina Botanical Garden
9 Savannah: Savannah Gardens
10 Statesboro: Georgia Southern University Botanical Garden
11 Fort Valley: Massee Lane Gardens
12 Pine Mountain: Callaway Gardens
13 Atlanta: Atlanta Botanical Garden
14 Atlanta: Atlanta History Center
15 Atlanta: Fernbank Science Center
16 Athens: Founders Memorial Garden
17 Athens: State Botanical Garden
18 Mount Berry: Oakhill
19 Huntsville: Huntsville-Madison County Botanical Garden
20 Birminham: Birmingham Botanical Garden
21 Montgomery: Jasmine Hill Gardens
22 Dothan: Dothan Area Botanical Gardens
23 Theodore: Bellingrath Gardens

DEEP SOUTH:

South Carolina, Georgia, Alabama

The Deep South—delineated here by the borders of South Carolina, Georgia, and Alabama—is a place steeped in the context of landscape. In some ways these states have always had a closer relationship with the land than most others. Beginning with the plantations, in which agriculture mixed with aristocracy to create places intimately connected with the land, and ending with today's botanical gardens that are fomenting a renewed interest in native plants, the story of gardens in this region seems to be one of trying to get closer to the real truth of the landscape—to understand and embody its spirit more fully. This is palpable at the plantation gardens around Charleston. At both Middleton Place and Magnolia Plantations southern aristocrats created a kind of landscape temple to honor and bolster their way of life. This can easily be read in the layout of slave quarters, in which power and freedom were retained in the main house and pleasure grounds immediately surrounding it but were stripped from the small barracks, lined up almost prisonlike in a neglected corner. But there's far more to the story than prejudice and slavery. The plantation owners had a strong sense of the landscape as a work of art in contrast with more mercantile societies (the North, for example) that might see the land as only in economic terms. At Middleton Place Henry Middleton made this amply clear with the amount of time, money, and labor he committed to accentuating the soulful character of the Ashley River.

The story of the Deep South is also a kind of march to the sea, in that the region encompasses, over a short distance, an important topographical shift from the Piedmont forests and mountains of Georgia to the lowland of South Carolina and Alabama's gulf coast. The botanical gardens of Georgia, in particular the wonderful natural gardens at Callaway, help us to understand ways that, while

OPPOSITE: *Callaway Gardens in Pine Mountain, Georgia*

DEEP SOUTH

ABOVE: *Atlanta Botanical Garden*

BELOW: *Magnolia Plantation in Charleston*

perhaps not new, have been forgotten. Callaway seems to say, as it did to its founder: "Stop. Take a look at this flower or this tree. This, more than anything, is Georgia." As in the rest of the South, there has been a strong movement toward native plants and ecological gardening in this region—again, particularly in Georgia. This is due in part to the existence of a major landscape architecture program at the university in Athens, and to indefatigable presence of Darrel Morrison, a professor there and one of the leaders in the field of ecological planting design.

Besides its botanical gardens, Alabama makes its mark with the estate gardens of Walter Bellingrath in Mobile. Here we come upon the gulf coast and a moment of transition from the east to the southern Midwest. But before we do, we linger a moment in the traditions of Europe and Asia that Bellingrath has so aptly imported to his tract along the Fowl River.

DEEP SOUTH: SOUTH CAROLINA

Murrells Inlet: Brookgreen Gardens

LOCATION: EIGHTEEN MILES SOUTH OF MYRTLE BEACH ON U. S. ROUTE 17

GARDEN OPEN: 9:30 am to 4:30 pm daily. Admission: nominal fee.

FURTHER INFORMATION FROM:
1931 Brookgreen Drive,
Murrells Inlet 29576
(843) 237-4218

NEARBY SIGHTS OF INTEREST:
Myrtle Beach, Huntington Beach

In the 1930s millionaire Archer Milton Huntington and his wife Anna purchased 9,000 acres of former rice plantation in order to create a sculpture park to display Anna's work. The landscape evolved over the years with the addition of hundreds of other pieces and now exists as a major attraction in the lowlands south of Myrtle Beach. The works are all representational. They include such artists as Daniel Chester French (sculptor of the Lincoln Memorial in Washington), Augustus Saint-Gaudens, and of course Huntington, whose tribute to Don Quixote is both sentimental and ironic. The grounds are landscaped to provide more than a backdrop to the art. The mature canopy, many streams, and lush understory of ornamental shrubbery all interact with the pieces, providing balance and dialogue. There are several iconic areas such as an airy allée of live oaks dripping with Spanish Moss. Water plays a major role throughout, enlivening much of the sculpture with reflective, dynamic counterpoint. In one instance it is used a plinth for a heroic piece carved classically in the round and raised within a dark stone basin. In another it provides a canvas for a playful piece, extending beyond the confines of the object to provide a landscape amenity for a wooden pergola and an effusion of perennials. An Italianate pool resides in the center of the garden and is a main feature for formal garden enthusiasts.

The sculpture of Anna Hyatt Huntington structures the horticultural display at Brookgreen Gardens.

2 Moncks Corner: Cypress Gardens

GARDEN OPEN: 9 am to 5 pm daily, except major holidays and the month of January.
ADMISSION: $7 adults, $5 seniors, $2 children.

FURTHER INFORMATION FROM:
3030 Cypress Gardens Road,
Moncks Corner 29461
(843) 553-0515

NEARBY SIGHTS OF INTEREST:
Nesbitt House, Berkeley Museum

LOCATION: OFF U. S. ROUTE 52, ON CYPRESS GARDENS ROAD, NORTH OF CHARLESTON

Cypress Gardens was once Dean Hall Plantation, a major rice farm on the Cooper River. Like so many other plantations Dean Hall fell into disrepair after the Civil War. The property was purchased in the 1920s by wealthy northerner William Kittredge who used it primarily for duck hunting. But lore has it that one day Kittredge fell in love with a single red maple leave shimmering in the water and decided to transform the wildlife reserve into an ornamental garden. He imported plants such as Daphne, fuschias, azaleas, and camellias, and paid local children to gather wild bulbs such as Atamasco lily and arranged them within the woods, mostly along the water's edge. The garden is primarily water-based and filled with primeval cypresses and an assortment of wildlife, including exotic ducks and plenty of alligators. And yet the primary way of viewing the garden is by bateaux, flat-bottomed boats that easily glide through the water. The river has a peculiar black tint, owing to the humus on the bottom, which has the magnificent effect of clearly reflecting the surrounding landscape much in the way that Kittredge witnessed it on his transformative day. Unfortunately much of Cypress Gardens was demolished during Hurricane Hugo in 1989. Almost 12,000 plants were lost, including many cypresses, forever altering the character of the land. The gardens were closed for several years while money poured in to restore them. In 1996 they were reopened, and reports say that the wildlife content is still amazing, although it was not possible to replicate Kittredge's amateurish, and hence beguiling, design. Nonetheless, the spirit of a naturalistic garden dedicated to the topography and botany of the lowlands remains. In addition to the gardens there is a butterfly house, including an exhibit of bees and arthropods (spiders, scorpions, and insects), and a swamp aquarium.

Flat-bottomed "bateaux" carry visitors into the depths of Cypress Gardens.

3 Hartsville: Kalmia Gardens of Coker College

LOCATION: TWO-AND-A-HALF MILES WEST OF HARTSVILLE ON STATE ROUTE 151, SIXTY MILES EAST OF COLUMBIA

These gardens adorn the oldest building in Hartsville, the nineteenth-century plantation house of Captain Thomas Hart. The property came into the hands of the Coker family, benefactors of the local college, in the 1930s. Miss May Coker was the garden maker and she transformed the 30-acre property into a naturalistic garden that eventually, like all of the estate, was donated to Coker College. The garden's main focus is on azaleas, camellias, and other ornamental shrubs and woody plants indigenous to this area. True to its name, there are some stunning examples of mountain laurel (*Kalmia latifolia*) which come to life in May, although their dainty architectural habitat is a subtle attribute of the woods throughout the year. The dramatically gorged Black Creek winds along one edge of the garden, and a precipitous 86-step wooden staircase brings non-wheelchair visitors down through the dense forest canopy to a pavilion that overlooks its banks, which after a heavy rain can flood. Adjoining the garden is the 700-acre Heritage-Segars Preserve of swampy cypress forest.

GARDEN OPEN: dawn to dusk daily. ADMISSION: free.

FURTHER INFORMATION FROM:
1624 West Carolina Avenue,
Hartsville 29550
(843) 383-8145
www.coker.edu/Kalmia

NEARBY SIGHTS OF INTEREST:
National Military Cemetery

DEEP SOUTH: SOUTH CAROLINA

Water is omnipresent at Middleton Place, and used to create floral displays.

5 Pinesville: Middleton Place

LOCATION: ON STATE ROUTE 61, FOURTEEN MILES NORTH OF CHARLESTON

GARDEN OPEN: 9 am to 5 pm daily, year-round. ADMISSION: $15 adults, $7 children.

FURTHER INFORMATION FROM: 4300 Ashley River Road, Charleston 29414
(800) 782-3608
www.middletonplace.org

NEARBY SIGHTS OF INTEREST: Fort Sumter National Monument

Middleton Place is the oldest continually maintained garden in America. Although the house burned down in the 1920s, the sumptuous landscape gardens have been well preserved, offering an incredible glimpse into the glamorous life of a plantation in the antebellum South. The design was shepherded by Henry Middleton beginning in the 1780s. Records show that Middleton hired a gardener in Charleston, although owing to the design it was probably an Englishman well schooled in Continental aesthetics. At the time European estates were following the lead of André Le Nôtre whose work at Versailles at the end of the seventeenth century had set the tone for large-scale landscape gardens. But as we move toward the nineteenth century, the strict geometry of the French garden was transformed across the channel into the picturesque, country parkland gardens of England. Middleton Place is caught between these two aesthetics. It employs a rigorous geometrical balance and several formal European gestures in its small gardens. However "the big move" on-site is fundamentally English. This is the cascading lawn terrace that rolls down to the Ashley River. A strong axis—formed at first by a paved terrace and then at the

The surrounding wilderness provides counterpoint.

Enormous live oaks provide backdrop and structure to classical arrangements.

bottom by a grass levee between two "butterfly-shaped" lakes—structures the immediate space. But the overall focus is on the surrounding, naturalistic vistas in which the lazy Ashley River is preeminent. This concern with the vista and the estate's relationship with it is essentially English, while the small gestures (the axis, for instance) may be French. The most striking component of this garden are the butterfly ponds, which one floats down to by way of a series of grass terraces joined by gentle grass ramps. A dedicated and intelligent maintenance crew keeps the turf well groomed so that the edges of the lakes and the precise but soft ramping of the lawn retain a sense of being cut from the landscape rather than placed upon it.

The house once stood in at the top of the terrace as if on a plinth, commanding an incredible view of the country. And it is just another indicator of the curious importance of Middleton Place, that even in the absence of the mansion the garden has been maintained. Adjacent to the house are several formal garden areas. These include the *Formal Garden* just to the northwest. This is fashioned as a set of parallel and perpendicular axes, defined by allées and pathways that set against one another to create small, grassy garden spaces. As it is situated atop the hill, the parterres frame, enclose, and then hide views of the river. Sculpture once adorned the garden but much of its was stolen during ransacking at the end of the Civil War. Today only a lonely wood nymph carved by Johann

The formal gardens use minimal planting to achieve a stately effect.

Rudolph Schadow remains. Close to the house were also a small sunken garden with a grass bowl at its bottom and the *Sundial Garden* with triangular beds of old variety roses. Enclosing the entire residential area of the plantation and acting as a barrier to the forest are two pools. One, the reflection pool, is a rigorously rectangular cut in the land surrounded by cool grass and a selection of flowering shrubs including crepe myrtle. The *Azalea Pool* has lost its geometric shape and is more flowing and naturalistic. The wooded edge is stuffed to the brim with a rainbow of azaleas. In the nineteenth century camellias were added to the landscape, and today many of these venerable remnants are gigantic, forming shaded tunnels of color foliage that run through the garden, making borders and edges to the space. But the king of old plants is the Middleton oak, an absolutely mind-blowing live oak located on a rise above the river, which botanists estimate to be 800 years old.

While structure, order, and large landscape ideas are what Middleton Place is known for, there is plenty of color in the garden. Tasteful arrangements of crocii and redbud grace the main allée; white lilies dance around the edge of the butterfly lakes; hydrangeas enliven the parterre in summer. A new garden of camellias has been organized beyond the *Formal Garden*. In addition, the entire forest is cut through with paths. It is a magnificent collection of trees including many kalmias, or mountain laurel, which are unusual in this climate.

Middleton Place claimed itself from the Ashley River through an artful system of levees and lakes.

DEEP SOUTH: SOUTH CAROLINA

GARDEN OPEN: 8:00 am to 5:00 pm daily, March–October; 8:30 am to 4:30 pm daily, November–February. **ADMISSION:** $10 adults, $9 seniors, $8 students, $5 children.

FURTHER INFORMATION FROM
3550 Ashley River Road,
Charleston 29414
(800) 367-3517
magnoliaplantation.net

NEARBY SIGHTS OF INTEREST
Fort Sumter National Monument

TOP: *Old azaleas lace the woods at Magnolia Plantation.*

BOTTOM: *Putti in the garden at Magnolia Plantation*

4 Charleston: Magnolia Plantation

LOCATION: U. S. ROUTE 17 SOUTH FROM DOWNTOWN, OVER THE ASHLEY RIVER BRIDGE, TO FIRST EXIT (STATE ROUTE 61), THEN TEN MILES NORTH

Magnolia Plantation has been the American headquarters for the Drayton family since the seventeenth century. Its rolling landscape and artful gardens are some of the oldest continually maintained in the country. And for visitors to Charleston there are few better ways to imbibe the antebellum spirit than here. Among all the politicians, businessmen, and financiers that the family spawned, the most influential, in terms of Magnolia itself, was Reverend John Grimke Drayton, an intellectual Episcopal minister who set about designing the landscape in the 1850s upon the example of English landscape practices of the time. John Drayton made several characteristic moves in the landscape such as locating groves and architectural structures to train views and create a sense of expansiveness and romance. The most outstanding example is the *long bridge*, a magnificent, low-arching wood bridge that spans a former rice paddy drained into a pond. Its purpose is less to walk across (although you can) than to be seen from a distance and to provide scale to the landscape. Drayton used azaleas (which he imported) and camellias liberally throughout his gardens to enliven the deep greenery, create edges, and form floral bosques. The oldest gardens on-site were actually planted by the first settlers on the land, Thomas Drayton and his wife Ann Fox, when they arrived from the British colony of Barbados in the 1680s. The garden is tropical in nature, evoking more the feeling of the Caribbean than Charleston. Besides the large landscape moves, John Drayton also built a maze garden based upon those of the English court. But instead of boxwood, Drayton used camellias (500 of them!) intermixed with hollies. The labyrinthine design is made doubly confusing by the overwhelming visual presentation of the plant material. The last garden to be made onsite is the *Biblical Garden*, constructed by modern-day gardeners interested in investigating plants of the Holy Land and making theological and historical connections. Thus we see bitter greens, frankincense, myrrh, carob, and tamarisk—all items mentioned in the scriptures, and definitely in abundance in ancient Israel. The design is divided into Old and New Testament areas, with Jewish icons adorning the former and Christian the latter. The plantation house is the third on the property, an earlier one having been burned by General Sherman's troops during the Civil War. Shortly after erecting this one, John Drayton opened the plantation to the public as a kind of living museum, thus making it the oldest public garden in the country.

5 Charleston: Heyward-Washington House

LOCATION: 87 CHURCH STREET, BETWEEN BROAD AND TRADD, JUST OFF THE BATTERY

GARDEN OPEN: 10 am to 5 pm Monday–Saturday, 1 pm to 5 pm Sunday, year-round.
ADMISSION: $7 adults, $4 children.

FURTHER INFORMATION FROM: 360 Meeting Street, Charleston 29403
www.charlestonmuseum.com

NEARBY SIGHTS OF INTEREST: Charleston Museum, the Battery, Joseph Manigault House

This historic house (1772) was the home of prominent Charlestonian Thomas Heyward Jr., a signer of the Declaration of Independence. It was even rented to George Washington when he visited the city in 1791. The house has been well maintained by the local museum and contains a wonderful collection of period furnishings. The gardens were planted in the 1930s in the colonial revival manner—meaning that they were intended to portray life during the eighteenth century but really reflect Victorian sensibilities of the late nineteenth century. The formal garden is a boxwood parterre enclosed by a terrace and filled with heirloom plants from the era. The most faithful "colonial" accouterment is the vegetable garden, which contains medicinal and household items, including flowers that were important for freshening things up inside the house.

An old time feel pervades the historic garden at the Heyward-Washington House.

DEEP SOUTH: SOUTH CAROLINA

GARDEN OPEN: dawn to dusk daily. **ADMISSION:** free.

FURTHER INFORMATION FROM:
1624 West Carolina Avenue,
Hartsville 29550
(843) 383-8145
www.coker.edu/Kalmia

NEARBY SIGHTS OF INTEREST:
National Military Cemetery

6 Columbia: Riverbanks Botanical Garden

LOCATION: JUST OFF INTERSTATE 126 AT GREYSTONE BOULEVARD, ON THE NORTHWEST SIDE OF DOWNTOWN

Riverbanks Botanical Garden was constructed in 1995 as a major addition to the Riverbanks Zoo, which already featured a wondrously maintained garden setting. The botanical garden offers a world of contrasts. The lowland portions of the 70-acre garden lie along the Saluda River and are intensely naturalistic. The bottoms and the slope feature a diverse collection of South Carolina hardwoods such as oaks and hickories. The ground plane, cut through by a matrix of trails, has been managed and planted with native flowering shrubbery, including wildflowers, mountain laurel, and plenty of Spanish moss. About 135 feet above the river, where the slope evens off, is an enormous walled garden. Visitors enter through a new visitors center and face a classically balanced garden with a central canal terminating in a gazebo—yet detailed and planted in a contemporary vein. The fountain at the end of the canal is surrounded by Australian cabbage trees, which lend a sense of funkiness to the otherwise formal setting. The collections, contained within brick-lined planters, adhere both to themes and simple beauty. There are several color-themed presentations as well as unusual displays of berries, luminescent plants, and an *Art Garden* where works of local sculptors are woven into a tapestry of floral color. At the far end of the garden lies a more informal collection of heirloom roses that provides a transition to a path that leads back to the woodland garden down below. Pittsburgh-based Environmental Planning and Design, one of the leading botanical garden design firms in the country, planned the gardens. Although it is a young garden, the designers were able to create the sense that it has always been there by using high quality stone and mature plants.

A 300-foot canal structures a walled garden at Riverbanks.

7 Clemson: South Carolina Botanical Garden

LOCATION: PERIMETER ROAD, OFF U.S. ROUTE 76, ON THE CLEMSON UNIVERSITY CAMPUS

GARDEN OPEN: dawn to dusk daily. ADMISSION: free.

FURTHER INFORMATION FROM:
130 Lehotsky Hall, Clemson University, Clemson 29634
(864) 656-3405

NEARBY SIGHTS OF INTEREST:
Sumter National Forest

The botanical garden at Clemson got its start as a scrappy little camellia collection clinging to the red clay of an old farmstead. The garden, in some ways, was developed as a strategy for reclaiming the land and restoring the topsoil that had been stripped away over the years. Because it is associated with a university, the facility has grown garden by garden, based upon donors and their interests. But in 1992 it became the state botanical garden, a designation that gives it more stability and assures its future. Befitting the name it is a sizable, diverse space containing smaller areas developed according to different ideas and themes. Public education plays a major role, and influenced the creation of the large demonstration garden of turf grass and common flowers. This area is laid out as a carpet of swirling colors cut into a gently lilting hillside. In addition to various annuals and perennials, the garden showcases uncommon turf grasses in order to give the everyday homeowner different ideas. Taking this concept much further is the *Xeriscape Garden,* where water-conserving and chemical independent landscape practices are displayed. Although Xeriscape gardens are typically thought of as arid, water is a major issue in the eastern United States, as the drought of 1999 showed. Following the ecological theme the *Bernice Dodgens Lark Wildflower Meadow* presents a layered tapestry of native wildflowers. The seed mix was designed by a graduate student at Clemson and cleverly arranged so that taller species are kept in the background while shorter ones remain up front. The wispy lobelia, shy dog lily, and rustic oconee bells are just some of the characters that show up here and along a wildflower trail that winds through the property. One of the highlights of the garden is the sculpture area. Instead of a garden-variety representative or abstract objects cast in metal or cut from stone, the works in this garden are all drawn from the traditions of earth art made in the 1970s, yet updated with a contemporary twist. Much of the work is student-generated and of a temporary nature, but there are also works by prominent artists such as Herb Parker, who is known for his sod houses.

South Carolina Botanical Garden's gentle terrain

9 Savannah: Savannah Gardens

LOCATION: DOWNTOWN SAVANNAH

GARDEN OPEN: Squares open all times; call historic houses for information. **ADMISSION:** varies for the historic houses.

FURTHER INFORMATION FROM: Garden Center, Savannah 31406 (912) 355-3883

NEARBY SIGHTS OF INTEREST: U. S. Customs House

Savannah's tree-lined and garden-bordered walks.

There aren't any gardens in Savannah. The entire city is a garden, a string of small parks and landscaped niches all of which are designed in the classic European formal style, with various amendments and add-ons that are mostly Georgian in flavor. The live oak is king here, with crepe myrtle, southern magnolias, and boxwood playing various dukes and duchesses. Radial designs are cut round with ancient boxwood and then graced by a canopy of gnarled oaks; the barest wisp of excitement in some spring bulbs or a flowering tree is a common trope. Wandering from one square to the next you will see this idea evolve and change. There are two reasons why the city is so gardenesque. One has to do with its deep, complex spirit, which has been probed by various writers and films of late. Another, more mundane reason relates to its plan, devised by colonial governor James Oglethorpe in the eighteenth century. Oglethorpe created a system of small squares that dotted a grid of streets. Not only did this slow things down in the core (alleys, the first in the country, were cut behind the building facades to facilitate movement) but it provided a neighborhood focal point: the perfect place for a garden park. In all there are 23 parks, each of which the local community has transformed into its little identity garden. Woven into the fabric are numerous house gardens, many of which are open to the public or can be glimpsed from the street. Although a visit to these gardens should also look to understand the entire city, there are some specific nodes within the fabric that bear mentioning and highlighting. The Davenport House (912-236-8097) on Habersham Street is a historic home and carriage house, dating to the nineteenth century, around which the most recent owners designed an intimate parterre garden with a fishpond. The space, little less than an acre, embodies the meticulous, detailed landscape that is so characteristic of Savannah. Another historic house is the Owens-Thomas House and Museum on Abercorn Street (912-233-9743) where in the 1950s garden designer Claremount Lee created a French-inspired parterre garden, rounded by narrow walking paths. The garden is still in good shape and features a grape arbor and a central reflecting pool. These houses, and many others, are merely formalized expressions of what occurs in Savannah everyday—people making gardens for public consumption. Unlike in the typical suburb, the urban gardens of Savannah are meant to be enjoyed by all. Homeowners and garden clubs showcase the splendor of the city rather than lock it away behind fences in a subdivision. Although Savannah is a small city, if one truly keeps one's eyes open to all its garden wonders, it could take days to get through.

Savannah's private gardens and public squares

GARDEN OPEN: Dawn to dusk daily, year-round.
ADMISSION: free.

FURTHER INFORMATION FROM:
Georgia Southern University,
P.O. Box 8039, Statesboro,
30460-8039
(912) 871-1114

NEARBY SIGHTS OF INTEREST:
Fort Stewart

10 Statesboro: Georgia Southern University Botanical Garden

LOCATION: TWELVE MILES NORTH OF INTERSTATE 16 VIA STATE ROUTE 67, TWO BLOCKS FROM CAMPUS

Dan Bland (known simply as Mr. Dan to most) began planting ornamentals and native trees on his farm in the 1920s; the juxtaposition between his agricultural and botanical roots run deep. In the 1980s he donated the farm to the local university for the purpose of establishing a botanical garden. Bland's original camellia garden has been well-tended over the years to produce an excellent collection of varieties that are native to this region of Georgia. The other vestige of Mr. Dan is a stately allée composed of southern magnolias and America holly, planted in double rows. Combined with a small assortment of partially restored outbuildings, this old geometry still speaks a farmer's language. In recent years the garden has made an effort to develop a series of ecological collections, such as the arboretum in a former parking lot. It includes plenty of magnolias, bayberry, hawthorn, and holly. There is also a bog garden planted with endangered pitcher plants. The main focus, a path first trod by Mr. Dan, is on native plant collections, and the woods are peppered with a wonderful collection of trees, understory plantings, and wildflowers all indigenous to the region. A significant gathering of woodland azaleas and rhododendrons was started several years ago. The garden is also contemplating the re-establishment of a pine savannah through the use of controlled burning.

Stoke's aster—a sample of the intrinsic beauty in the southern woods at Georgia Southern Botanical Garden

11 Fort Valley: Massee Lane Gardens

LOCATION: OFF STATE ROUTE 49 (EXIT 46 ON INTERSTATE 75), TWENTY MILES SOUTH OF MACON

GARDEN OPEN: 9 am to 5 pm Monday–Saturday, 1 pm to 5 pm Sunday, January–March; 9 am to 4 pm Monday–Friday, April–December. ADMISSION: $3 adults.

FURTHER INFORMATION FROM: 100 Massee Lane, Fort Valley 31030
(912) 967-2358

NEARBY SIGHTS OF INTEREST: Jarrell Plantation, Andersonville National Historic Site

Camellias were introduced in this country in the late eighteenth century when John Stevens of Hoboken, New Jersey, imported a single red *Camellia japonica* from England. At that time they were exclusively hothouse plants, shown in the greenhouses of wealthy northerners and at flower shows in Boston and Philadelphia. Eventually camellias made their way south where they could grow naturally in the gardens of Georgia and Florida; and by the twentieth century this colorful plant had become all but synonymous with the antebellum South. Dave Strother, a local oil baron, fell in love with camellias, and following a disastrous storm in the 1950s transformed his Fort Valley peach farm into a camellia garden. The garden has since become the home of the American Camellia Society, and today showcases the very latest in camellia science in its acres of test plots and formal gardens. Camellias are winter blooming, and so the gardens are in their glory from January to March. The highlight is the geometrically arranged formal camellia garden. In recent years the garden has expanded its horizons to roses and a Japanese garden that features a small woodland pool encapsulated with mondo grass and stepping stones. The newest addition is the environmental garden, which features plants native to this region of Georgia. Throughout the garden you will see granite gristmill stones that Strother rescued from a historic mill in central Georgia. Their corrugated, rough faces and perfectly rounded edges provide an interesting architectural counterpoint to the wonderfully lush southern hues of the camellias.

Camellias in full glory from January to March

DEEP SOUTH: GEORGIA

FALLS CREEK LAKE
GOLF COURSE
MR. CASON'S VEGETABLE GARDEN
VICTORY GARDEN SOUTH
BEACH ENTRANCE
MOUNTAIN CREEK LAKE
MOUNTAIN CREEK BOATHOUSE
RESTAURANT
INFORMATION CENTER
CECIL B. DAY BUTTERFLY CENTER
ROBIN LAKE

DEEP SOUTH: GEORGIA

12 Pine Mountain: Callaway Gardens

LOCATION: U. S. ROUTE 27 (EXIT 14 ON I-185), SOUTH OF PINE MOUNTAIN

Callaway Gardens, like most exceptional places, began as an idea inspired by the landscape. The idea blossomed with Cason and Virginia Callaway, a wealthy Georgia couple, as they were picnicking in the forest: Cason spied a beautiful flower; he thought it was a "wild honeysuckle," but Virginia did some research and discovered it was a *Rhododendron prunifolium*, a native Georgian azalea. So enamored by the beauty of the surrounding landscape, they purchased the land and set about planting a wonder garden of azaleas. Much has happened since then: Callaway Gardens has evolved into a family resort, with golf, water-skiing, and an assortment of recreational opportunities. The gardens have also evolved to become one of the most prominent horticultural destinations in the country.

Rather than a single, unified garden, Callaway Gardens is actually a group of separate gardens located within the 14,000-acre complex and connected by a system of trails. At the center of the fuss is Cason Callaway's *Vegetable Garden*, an enormous seven-and-a-half-acre plot, planted with an array of regional crops. Although mundane-sounding, the vegetable garden is both a horticultural and artistic delight, showcasing a keen sensitivity to native plants and a taste for employing fruits and vegetables into an eclectic assemblage of colors, textures, and smells. The upper terrace of the garden contains blueberries, muscadine grapes, and other unusual creeping edibles. Below this is more standard fare: tomatoes, squash, beans, and such southern favorites as okra, field peas, and collard greens, much of which are used in the restaurant on the grounds. The last terrace features herbs and fruits trees. The entire display acts as a living laboratory for various botanical trials and testing. Most recently a patch of wildflowers was cultivated for a brief time—intriguingly in a non-naturalistic style. Adjacent to the Vegetable Garden is the *Meadowlark Gardens* area. Lying along the side of the Mountain Creek Lake, this part of Callaway features three distinct plant collections, wildflowers, hollies, and rhododendrons, all planted in woodland settings. The rhododendrons are all broadleaf varieties lying at the southern extent of their range, intermixed with various heathers, and underplanted with ferns and lily-of-the-valley to create a multilayered, dense presentation. The *Wildflower Trail* winds through several habitat associations, including a bog, coastal plain, and piedmont, which helps to expand the wildflower vocabulary beyond just woodlands and meadows. Among more familiar naturalized varieties, several rare and endangered species are found here. Each of these walking trail gardens is situated around the *Cecil B. Day Butterfly Center*, designed by Henri V. Jova of Atlanta, an enormous octagonal glass structure that contains

GARDEN OPEN: 9 am to 5 pm Monday–Saturday, 1 pm to 5 pm Sunday, January–March; 9 am to 4 pm Monday–Friday, April–December. ADMISSION: $3 adults.

FURTHER INFORMATION FROM: 100 Massee Lane, Fort Valley 31030
(912) 967-2358

NEARBY SIGHTS OF INTEREST: Jarrell Plantation, Andersonville National Historic Site

OPPOSITE: *The stained-glass windows of Fay Jones' Gothic-inspired chapel feature native plants found in the woods.*

over 1,000 butterflies and several types of ground and water birds. Among the exotic fauna are rare African butterflies. The landscape was designed by Robert Marvin, a famous designer from the lowlands of South Carolina, and features a 12-foot waterfall and a lush palette of tropical plants. Outside the structure lies a wildlife garden planted to attract native butterflies, hummingbirds, and other wonderful creatures. It also serves to make connections between the rather esoteric world inside and the exciting world outside.

Farther along, stalwart garden visitors will come to the *Ida Cason Callaway Chapel*, a Gothic styled church built out of native Georgian fieldstone and red oak. Cason Callaway designed and built the church to honor his mother, and also to

make a strong but subtle statement about God and nature. Note the six stained-glass windows executed by Joel Reeves that depict plants in the local woods. The four west windows represent the seasons in the gardens, the south window depicts the pine evergreen forest of Georgia's coastal plain, while the northern window represents the hardwood forest of the Georgia's northern Piedmont plant community. Beyond the chapel lies the extraordinary *John A. Sibley Horticultural Center*. Named after a local civic leader and friend of the Callaways, the center was built in 1984 in a very nontraditional manner. The whole idea was that typical conservatories perform the ironic task of presenting a view of nature while at the same time shutting it out. Robert Marvin, in particular, has been eloquent about this tendency not just in greenhouses but in all parts of our lives. In response his landscape design (architects for the structure were Craig, Gualden and Davis from Greenville, South Carolina) opens up the conservatory and lets the landscape flow into and through the structure. Smart siting orients the building so that severe temperature fluctuations are eliminated in the inner recesses, a healthy climate for common glasshouse plants—Benjamin ficus, raphis palm, tree ferns, holly ferns, and dastiron plants. Moving toward the perimeter, the landscape becomes more subtropical, and then finally a Georgian display where ferns and camellias interplay with a rock wall. Many of the permanent plants in the collection are considered "border-line" hardy for

the garden. The effect is transcendent, allowing one to palpably understand the essence of a conservatory and the hints of what we might see in a more progressive future. The structure itself is remarkable. The rock walls are Tennessee fieldstone; the translucent roof is a silicone-coated fiberglass fabric.

The inspiration for Callaway was, and in some ways remains, azaleas. For many years the *Azalea Trail* has been the main place to view azaleas. It features a wide range of azaleas in a natural woodland setting, complemented by red maples and naturalized bulbs. In 1999, however, Callaway opened the *Callaway Brothers Azalea Bowl*, billed as the largest azalea garden in the world. The collection of 4,000 plants includes both natives and hybrids and covers 40 acres. It was designed by Tom Wirth of Massachusetts who worked with the garden's original pattern of planting around water features to enhance the spectacular color of the plants. The collection features both natives and Kurumes. The rest of the landscape beyond these separate gardens is given over to miles of walking trails through the same magical landscape that beguiled Callaway fifty years ago. There are many additions, such as a golf resort and a railroad, that intrude upon the pure aesthetic. But the gardens are still well-tended and feature some of the most marvelous displays in the entire region.

OPPOSITE, TOP: *A thousand exotic butterflies inhabit a specially designed habitat.*

OPPOSITE, MIDDLE: *Water features traditionally enhance the superlative nature of native azaleas.*

OPPOSITE, BOTTOM: *Many Vegetable Garden products find their way into the Calaway restaurant.*

The Vegetable Garden harvest

GARDEN OPEN: dawn to dusk daily. **ADMISSION:** $10 adults; $5 children.

FURTHER INFORMATION FROM:
P.O. Box 2000
Pine Mountain, GA 31822
800-Callaway
www.callawaygardens.com

NEARBY SIGHTS OF INTEREST:
Columbus Confederate Naval Museum, Little White House State Historic Site

Ecological displays, such as this bog garden of carnivorous pitcher plants, are part of the garden's program.

13 Atlanta: Atlanta Botanical Garden

LOCATION: PIEDMONT AVENUE, BETWEEN 14TH STREET AND MONROE DRIVE, JUST NORTH OF DOWNTOWN

Piedmont Park has been an impromptu gathering place for gardeners over the last forty years. In the 1960s a group of rose enthusiasts planted a rose garden. A little later a small Japanese garden came to life. Then an eighteenth-century herb knot. Finally, in the 1970s the Atlanta Botanical Garden was organized, based around these few disparate gardens. Since then it has grown into a significant civic amenity. The three original gardens still occupy the heart of the garden. The herb garden is a tight, brick-walled space with a thick knot of rosemary and sage, bordered by dwarf boxwood and anchored by a sundial. Surrounding this central design are beds with culinary, medicinal, and other kinds of herbs arranged as specimens with adequate labeling. The *Japanese Garden* has been well maintained over the years. It is green based, with pines and grass forming the canvas, with a carefully arranged overlay of flowering trees and bamboo. Architectural features such as stone lanterns and small bridges train views. Native plants and ecological gardens have become a more contemporary focus. A *bog garden* contains a wild assortment of carnivorous plants, such as pitcher plants and butterwort that trap insects in their tightly clawed "mouths." The *Upper Woodland* is designed as a series of displayed collections, including hardy camellias and a fern glade where the full spectrum of frondy ferns is arranged in a kind of march to the sea based on their geological origin, moving horizontally from mountainous to coastal types. In 1989 this rather young garden received a major boost when a local philanthropist donated the capital for a conservatory. Designed by Heery Architects and Engineers, the conservatory houses a large display of tropical plants and wildlife. The palms form the backbone, but unlike most glasshouses, Old World varieties from Madagascar are featured. There is also a significant collection of ferns and epiphytes (such plants that grow in trees as Spanish moss). More than 1,000 orchids complete the array with a beautiful flourish. Reflective of its strong public education mission, the garden has recently added a large children's garden to its repertoire. Along with all the flashy, playful bug and animal figures so common to children's gardens, this one features an unusual programmatic element: a planting theme that concentrates on plants that contribute to wellness and health.

DEEP SOUTH: GEORGIA

14 Atlanta: Atlanta History Center

LOCATION: CORNER OF SLATON DRIVE AND WEST PACES FERRY ROAD, NORTH OF DOWNTOWN.

The Atlanta History Center is a collection of modern and historic buildings—some, such as the Tullie Smith Farm (circa 1845) actually embody history, while others are used to store and display collections. The entire complex is located on a 33-acre tract of land that features several gardens. The spiritual center of the place is the *Swan House Garden*, which adorns a 1926 manor designed by local Atlanta architect Philip Trammell Shutze. While the house reflects an English country estate sensibility, Shutze gave the gardens a classically Italian cast. The architectural features are stunning and wear the patina of old age with grace. The main parterre of boxwood, which is designed with a strong central spine that culminates in a ringed fountain, has recently been completely restored. Overlaid upon these bones are seasonal plantings of candytuft, caladiums, and lambs ear that soften and deepen the mood. The foil to the Italianate rigor of the Swan House Garden is the distinctly naturalistic *Quarry Garden*. It features a well-tended and smartly crafted display of woodland plants—many of which are endangered wild varieties—set into a quiet, abandoned quarry. The space was discovered in the 1970s when the museum was looking to expand. Sensing its magical qualities a group of dedicated garden volunteers argued that it should be enhanced as a garden rather than torn out for redevelopment. In the spring the garden comes alive with trillium, violets,

GARDEN OPEN: 10:00 am to 5:00 pm Monday–Saturday, noon to 5:30 pm Sunday, year-round. ADMISSION: $10 adults, $8 seniors and students, $6 children

FURTHER INFORMATION FROM: 130 West Paces Ferry Road, Atlanta 30305
(404) 814-4000
www.atlantahistory.net

NEARBY SIGHTS OF INTEREST: Collanwolde Fine Arts Center, Governor's Mansion

The Swan House features a classical Italianate garden designed by Philip Trammell Shutze.

bloodroot, and bluebells, which drift overtop of the old, worn architecture of carved rock. Also located at the *History Center* is a re-created farm garden that adorns a relocated farmhouse, the *Tullie Smith Farm*. It contains all varieties of domestic herbs and flowers, as well as a working garden of vegetables. Located near McElreath Hall is an Asian themed garden of Japanese maples set around a lovely little gazebo that echoes the romanticism of Shutze's Swan House. (It was designed by a protégé.) An interesting twist to the gardens was added in 1993 when the center commissioned Darrel Morrison, a landscape architect and professor at University of Georgia, to design a sustainable garden entrance. Morrison divided the area into five zones that reveal the regional landscape types, including an outcrop garden of granite reflective of the native Piedmont stone and several pine groupings. The garden is maintained without the use of chemicals and irrigation, and thus assumes a rough character at times, which over the years has made it somewhat controversial.

15 Atlanta: Fernbank Science Center

LOCATION: PONCE DE LEON TO ARTWOOD ROAD, ON NORTH SIDE OF CITY

GARDEN OPEN: 2 pm to 5 pm Sunday–Friday, 10 am to 5 pm Saturday, year-round.
ADMISSION: free.

FURTHER INFORMATION FROM:
156 Heaton Park Drive, NE,
Atlanta 30307
(404) 378-4311
www.fsc.fernbank.edu

NEARBY SIGHTS OF INTEREST:
Fernbank Museum of Natural History

When it came to light several years ago that Atlanta residents enjoy the second longest commute in the country—a whopping 35 minutes average—it was just a statistical indicator of what everyone knew all along: sprawl was becoming a problem. Located in the heart of it all is Fernbank, a seventy-acre tract of old-growth forest that was wisely preserved back in 1939. At that time Emily Harrison who had a vision of using the land as a science education facility owned the property. It took almost thirty years for that to finally happen, but in 1967 the Fernbank Science Center opened. The landscape is integrated with the center's mission, and the forest that surrounds the center is indisputably its greatest asset. (The center's inclusion in this book as a "garden" is done with a view to its importance to the surrounding urban and suburban context.) It is a mixed association of hardwoods indigenous to the Piedmont region. A mile and half of trails wind through a cathedral of trees, with a fine-leafed understory and scores of wildflowers. Immediately behind the center is a home demonstration garden containing a vegetable garden, a butterfly garden, and a collection of native plants that are appropriate for the suburban yard. The central feature, however, is a composting area that serves the center and is also "daylighted" for public viewing as an educational exhibit. The center oversees two gardens offsite. The *Staton Rose Garden* is located at the Museum of Natural History at 767 Clifton Road. It was originally planted

in 1983 and has a strong horticultural bent, with many experimental specimens. There are also two Lord and Burnham greenhouses from the 1920s, where the center houses its small collection of tropicals and desert succulents; it is located at 1256 Briarcliff Road. The structures were renovated in the 1980s and are now used primarily for educational programs with the local school system.

The rose garden at Fernbank contrasts with the ecologically rich arboretum.

16 Athens: Founders Memorial Garden

LOCATION: AT THE SCHOOL OF ENVIRONMENTAL DESIGN, UNIVERSITY OF GEORGIA

The Founders Garden was designed and planted in 1946, to commemorate the 1891 founding of the Athens Ladies Garden Club, the first such club in America. The garden adorns an 1857 residence that had served many functions over the years, but now houses offices for the school of landscape architecture. The gardens are quite formal, reflecting the club's Victorian roots; although there are some newer areas that indicate a growing interest in more contemporary trends such as ecologi-

GARDEN OPEN: dawn to dusk daily. **ADMISSION:** free.

FURTHER INFORMATION FROM:
2450 Milledge Avenue,
Athens 30602
(706) 227-5369
www.uga.edu/gardenclub/Founder.html

NEARBY SIGHTS OF INTEREST:
University of Georgia

cal gardening. The *Boxwood Garden* is the main attraction at the garden, embodying its aesthetic soul. It is a small space enclosed by a white picket fence and described by rings of concentric boxwood and bands of red brick terrace. A sundial resides in the center, and in the middle of the beds formed in boxwood various perennials bloom in the spring. Around the edge is an overstuffed perennial border richly planted with period (1840) varieties, and at the far end, presiding over the time capsule of a landscape, is a small smokehouse. Beyond this garden, defined by the residence, are a small courtyard and terrace garden, the second more formal and open to the sun than the other. Both are fine architectural statements, with stone pavers rescued from a historic street in Athens by the dean of the landscape architecture school. Potted plants add a Mediterranean flair. The last formal garden area is a perennial border garden, arranged around a central path with old-time varieties such as phlox, foxglove, and roses. An arboretum of trees flushes through the rear part of the property, and has been transformed into a useful landscape for the botany department. The garden has now become a central feature of the design school, and because it is meant to remain a keepsake of a former era helps to steady the perambulations of undergraduates as they ramble forth on new adventures.

GARDEN OPEN: 8 am to 8 pm daily, April–September; 8 am to 6 pm daily, October–March.
ADMISSION: free.

FURTHER INFORMATION FROM:
2450 S. Milledge Avenue,
Athens 30605
(706) 542-1244
www.uga.edu/botgarden

NEARBY SIGHTS OF INTEREST:
University of Georgia

17 Athens: State Botanical Garden

LOCATION: ONE MILE FROM U. S. ROUTE 441, THREE MILES FROM UNIVERSITY OF GEORGIA'S ATHENS CAMPUS

The University of Georgia runs this botanical garden, and while such academic pursuits as research are an important component, the garden is oriented toward the general public. As such it has a public education feel to it. There are few formal garden areas; instead the rooms are predominantly theme oriented, to teach us about plants. The *International Garden,* lying just beyond the visitor center, is a kind of museum of plants. There are eleven different collections that depict the geographic origin of many plants and their cultural context, such as a medieval herb knot, collections of exotics from the far east, and an *Endangered Species Garden,* reflecting contemporary garden issues. The focus, of course, is on the thrilling traditions of plant exploration and discovery, and the great American plant hunters—such as John Bartram, his son William, and Ernest Henry Wilson—are all immortalized here. There are several other theme gardens, such as are found in most botanical gardens. The large and well-managed Annual and Perennial Garden leans more heavily toward the former rather than the latter, and the Shade Garden breaks out of the mold of a small bower and features an extensive stroll through a canopied forest, enlivened by a whole host of flowering shrubs. Azaleas, as can be expected, are rife through the garden, and the native azalea collection is one of the more popular destinations during the spring. Besides well-known varieties arranged in an elongated blooming cycle, the garden showcases many rare and endangered species in tribute to the great azalea authority Fred C. Galle. The garden has become increasingly focused on native plants and endangered plants and, besides the small display in the International Garden, sponsors the Georgia Endangered Plant Stewardship Network, which assists people with building and tending their own endangered plant gardens. The visitor's center was designed by Norris Hall and Marsh Architects and built in 1984. It houses a small conservatory filled with tropical plants.

ABOVE: *Mathis Plaza, LaGrazia Dello Stelo*

BELOW: *Fall foliage along the Orange trail*

18 Mount Berry: Oakhill, the Martha Berry Museum

LOCATION: VETERANS MEMORIAL HIGHWAY (U.S. ROUTE 1) AT U.S. ROUTE 27, JUST NORTH OF ROME

GARDEN OPEN: 10 am to 5 pm Monday–Saturday, 1 pm to 5 pm Sunday, year-round.
ADMISSION: $4 adults, $2 children.

FURTHER INFORMATION FROM:
P.O. Box 490189,
Mt. Berry 30149
(800) 220-5504
www.berry.edu/oakhill

NEARBY SIGHTS OF INTEREST:
Chattahoochee National Forest

Martha Berry grew up wealthy, but lived her life as an idealist. Unmarried, she converted her dowry, a parcel of land in the Georgia woods, into a school for poor mountain children. Her endeavors caught the attention of presidents and financiers (not necessarily in that order) and over her seventy years, Berry developed her little school house into a girls' school, and finally a college that, more than any well-intentioned government program, brought "book learning" to Appalachia. The campus finally encompassed many thousands of acres, but immediately around her house Berry developed a garden landscape, including some of the most precious formal gardens in the state. Berry's sister, Francis Rhea Berry, designed the Formal Garden. It is a rectangle drawn by a flagstone walkway lined with old boxwood. A French fountain marks the center of the garden and reflecting pool, vaguely framed by weeping specimen trees. At the outer edge of the grass panel that encompasses the fountain are bedded-out annuals in a colorful "draped cord" patterns. The Goldfish Garden is a tightly compressed secret garden of sorts. The focus is placed upon a central square of water, filled of course, with goldfish and buffered by an effusion of purple impatiens. The outer edge of the garden is equipped for meditation with a circle of benches. The Sundial Garden has more in common with a cloister garden than the Elizabethan form normally associated with the trope. Circular in composition, it features two bands of roses situated

Nodes, such as this secret garden, give the landscape a narrative quality.

around a central dial. The effect of the roses, which are cut back most of the year and thinly presented the rest of the time, is to open the space up. Rather than dark, brooding, and secretive, this garden is plainly visible, comprehensible, and hence slightly less interesting than it might possibly be. A personal favorite is the *Sunken Terrace Garden* designed by Martha Berry in 1932. It features a semicircular water feature built in old brick. The plaza makes a thin cut around the water, which has the effect of pushing the space out into the surrounding woods. It is a tense feeling that wakes the form from its sleepy Victorian grave and gives it an unusual modern interpretation. The last formal garden space is the *Bridal Walk*, a long arbor of old-time roses that ends at a gazebo. It is said that when Mrs. Berry's students were to be married she took them for a little walk out to the gazebo to make a wish.

19 Huntsville: Huntsville-Madison County Botanical Garden

LOCATION: BOB WALLACE DRIVE, EXIT 15 ON INERSTATE 565, EAST OF THE SPACE CENTER

Huntsville is most famous for the NASA center nearby; however this garden has a much more grounded view. And by combining artful formal gardens with a natural landscape focus, it succeeds in keeping our attention on Alabama rather than the sky. The central corridor provides the spine of the garden. A green alléeof grass is the focal point for a series of border gardens, most designed according to a theme or color scheme. A small *cottage garden* of such old-time favorites as verbena, asters, and phlox sweeps through an intimate space of two axial walkways ending in matching arbors. The circular *Aquatic Garden,* located at the end of the corridor, has a 110-wide lily pond at its center. A large viewing pavilion has been built out over the water, which is filled with a variety of naturalized water plants. The garden is rimmed with a woodland, part of which has been developed into a dogwood strolling area, featuring a 100-year-old specimen that was saved during a municipal road expansion. Visitors will also want to check out the *fern garden*, where over 170 different species are on display. Other garden areas include a classically *knotted herb garden*, a *vegetable demonstration garden*, and a 675-cultivar *daylily garden*.

GARDEN OPEN: 8:00 am to 6:30 pm Monday–Saturday, 1:00 pm to 6:30 pm Sunday, May–October; 9 am to 5 pm Monday–Saturday, 1 pm to 5 pm Sunday, November–April.
ADMISSION: $4 adults, $3 seniors, $2 students.

FURTHER INFORMATION FROM:
4747 Bob Wallace Avenue, Huntsville 35805
(205) 830-4447
www.hsvbg.org

NEARBY SIGHTS OF INTEREST:
Burritt Museum, U.S. Space and Rocket Center

20 Birmingham: Birmingham Botanical Gardens

GARDEN OPEN: dawn to dusk daily, year-round.
ADMISSION: free.

FURTHER INFORMATION FROM:
2612 Lane Park Road,
Birmingham 35223
(205) 879-1227
www.bbgardens.org

NEARBY SIGHTS OF INTEREST:
Southern Museum of Flight

LOCATION: OFF U. S. ROUTE 280, JUST SOUTH OF THE CITY

This is a handsome, small botanical garden that attempts to be both educational and beautiful—in fact it doesn't see these as necessarily contradictory. The southern ambience is set by the visitor center, a classic, double-porched residence rimmed with iron railings and framing a Mediterranean-style courtyard filled with tasteful contemporary sculpture. Immediately within lies the rose garden, a rectangular garden accessed through a whitewashed gate. A major destination within the garden is the Japanese area, marked by a brilliant red gate and laid out as a viewing garden of artfully placed rocks, dwarf conifers, and subtly colored ornamentals. There is also a small conservatory filled with palms and other tropicals. The most meditative room is undoubtedly the reflective pool garden. The terrace is bleached white, with a distinctive, altarlike portico at one end. The pool is carved into the ground plane in a perfectly proportioned rectangle of still water and dappled with a few reeds. The demonstration garden of herbs and flowers is set around a grass terrace, a woodland garden with wildflowers such as lobelia, and a park landscape of walking paths lined with crepe myrtle.

21 Montgomery: Jasmine Hill Gardens and Outdoor Museum

GARDEN OPEN: 9 am to 5 pm Tuesday–Sunday, year-round.
ADMISSION: $5 adults, $3 children.

FURTHER INFORMATION FROM:
P. O. Box 210792,
Montgomery 36121
(334) 567-6463
www.jasminehill.org

NEARBY SIGHTS OF INTEREST:
Montgomery Museum of Fine Arts

LOCATION: JASMINE HILL ROAD, NORTH OF THE CITY ON U. S. ROUTE 231

Jasmine Hill bills itself as "Alabama's little corner of Greece," by which it means to publicize the fact that its "outdoor museum" is an eclectic assemblage of Greek artifacts. Statues of Olympian discus throwers, crumbling colonnades, and other sculptural pieces are woven in a floral landscape of garden rooms, terraces, and intimate spaces. The approach is less horticultural or even formal than it is focused upon the idea of creating an enlivened canvas for these works of art. Some of the most prized places within the garden include: a reproduction of Winged Victory presiding over a small reflecting pool; a terrace planted with foxglove and other heirloom perennials; and the haunting ruins of fluted columns that stand sentinel over an opening in the landscape. The gardens are the brainchild of Ben and Mary Fitzpatrick and are now seventy-five years old. The graceful tufts of impatiens, celosia, and begonias are annual additions, while the mature bougainvillea, crepe myrtle, and phlox show the strong patina of age.

22 Dothan: Dothan Area Botanical Gardens

LOCATION: HOUSTON COUNTY ROAD 105, JUST OFF ROUTE U. S. 431 NORTH, NEAR LANDMARK PARK

GARDEN OPEN: dawn to dusk daily. ADMISSION: free.

FURTHER INFORMATION FROM:
5130 Headland Avenue,
Dothan 36301
(334) 793-3224
www.dabg.com

NEARBY SIGHTS OF INTEREST:
Boll Weevil Monument

This botanical garden is just a decade old, yet because it has been pushing forward with its concept plan, the *Rose Garden* and *Herb Garden* are the beginnings of acres of what will soon be garden rooms evolving into one another. Each garden is an enclosed, architecturally defined space. The Rose Garden is cupped in a rectangular brick enclosure and laid out with a central axis with smaller rectangular plots organized on a grid and a single border wrapping its way around the perimeter. The entrances are painted over with creepers that imbue the scientific presentation with romance. The Herb Garden is also a red-bricked structure and is defined as a square with raised radial beds overstuffed with medicinal and culinary herbs. A good herb garden needs to be intimate in order to concentrate the olfactory experience, and this one does a fine job. The center of the space is organized around a circular pool with four quiet benches that provide one of the more meditative places in the larger landscape. Recent additions to the garden include trails through the woodlands embracing the site. The trails are generally naturalistic, although some are peppered with wildflowers. The *Demonstration Garden* is another newcomer. Tended by local gardening superstars, this area is given over to vegetables and native plants that visitors might want to use in their own gardens. Besides champion pumpkins, the garden features lighter touches such as tufts of California poppies that encircle an edge or the display of muscadine grapes. The initial structures in the garden are intended to evoke southern charm. A small Victorian gazebo looks lazily over the Rose Garden, the entrance gate is constructed in old red brick to give a vaguely antebellum feel. But the focus of the garden is determinedly set upon the future. Bolstered by a small army of volunteers and donors it should complete its plan early in the new millennium.

An Alabama darkness descends around a fountain at the Dothan Area Botanical Garden

DEEP SOUTH: ALABAMA

23 Theodore: Bellingrath Gardens

LOCATION: BELLINGRATH ROAD, OFF U.S. ROUTE 90, TWENTY MILES SOUTHWEST OF MOBILE

GARDENS OPEN: 8 am to dusk daily. House open: 9 am to dusk daily. **ADMISSION** to gardens, house, and riverboat cruise: $18.95 adults, $13.95 children.

FURTHER INFORMATION FROM:
12401 Bellingrath Gardens Road
Theodore, AL 36582
(334) 973-2217
www.bellingrath.org/gardens

NEARBY SIGHTS OF INTEREST:
Fine Arts Museum of the South

BELOW, TOP: *Walter Bellingrath's prized possession—his gardens—wind magically around his home on the gulf coast.*

BOTTOM: *Wildlife seem to enjoy the artful presentation.*

The mythos of Walter Duncan Bellingrath's imperturbable industriousness centers around the image of a smiling young man carrying bottles of Coca Cola from town to town in the early years of the century. Such a work ethic, combined with a gentle character (so the story goes), helped Bellingrath build the first Mobile bottling company, which over the years amassed him a considerable fortune. When the doctor finally told him to relax, Bellingrath retreated to the steamy lowlands south of Mobile to a little fishing camp on Fowl River. Here he and his wife, Bessie Mae Morse, built a large house to accommodate their friends and family, surrounded by acres of glorious gardens. The formal center is the *South Terrace* and surrounding areas, designed in neoclassical style by architect George B. Meyers, whom Bellingrath enlisted to create the house and property. Most popular with wedding parties, the South Terrace features a stunning area of low lying pool fountains, intimately differentiated by overhanging trees and Spanish moss. A lack of shrubbery allows excellent views from one pool to the next and finally out to a majestic lawn that serves as a backdrop. Bellingrath died in the 1950s, preceded by his wife a decade earlier. The planting scheme tends towards the effusive: extreme contrasts of blooming azaleas and annuals overlaying the architectural structure of the garden. Sometimes this method can cave in upon itself, such as in the *Japanese Garden* where a small bridge over a lake—meant, in the tradition, to focus the eye and give the garden a diorama-like character—is overwhelmed by an incongruous heaping of daisies.

The garden generally becomes less formal farther from the house. An ecological boardwalk over the Fowl River is a new attraction that offers a unique chance to absorb the bayou context that Bellingrath determinedly rejected in his gardens. Wildlife is abundant here, including occasional alligators. The Bellingrath House contains many rare furnishings, and a former garage now houses a museum of the works of porcelain artist Edward Marshall Boehm.

Middleton Place reaches out to the Ashley River in Charleston.

1. Eureka Springs: Eureka Springs Gardens
2. Hot Springs: Garvan Woodland Gardens
3. Jackson: Mynelle Gardens
4. Picayune: Crosby Arboretum
5. Shreveport: American Rose Center
6. Many: Hodges Garden
7. Saint Francisville: Afton Villa
8. Baton Rouge: Hilltop Arboretum
9. New Orleans: New Orleans Botanical Garden
10. New Orleans: Long Vue
11. New Orleans: Garden District
12. Avery Island: Jungle Gardens
13. New Iberia: Rip Van Winkle Gardens

DELTA REGION:
Arkansas, Mississippi, Louisiana

Most people assume Delta refers to only the distinctly fingerlike spreading of the Mississippi River into the Gulf of Mexico. But in this book we refer to the *entire* delta, a complex river system that extends northward from Louisiana into Mississippi and Arkansas. The river not only affects the way of life here; it *is* the way of life. And whether one realizes it or not, everything—the climate, the economy, the culture, the history—of this region in some way, sooner or later, like water in a watershed, finds its way to the Mississippi.

Curiously, few of the gardens in this chapter directly relate to the Mississippi River. The plantations north of Baton Rouge come closest. Afton Villa is indisputably the king of these. Although the original house and gardens are gone, the twentieth-century efforts of the Trembles is absolutely extraordinary. There is both a sense for tradition and a sense of the new. We see the parterre carved in European fashion, and we see the native plants organized with a sense of ecology. But most characteristically what we see are the layers of history, the ruins of the house and gardens overlaid with new designs that don't replicate and don't erase what was there previously. It all works together into a rich pastiche—much like the river itself seems to embody and contain the spirit of the entire region.

Maybe this is stretching it a bit. But as we enter the basin of the Atchafalaya, and come upon the gardens of Avery and Jefferson Islands, connections with the mighty water system are undeniable. Each of these gardens occupies an island formed by salt domes that push the land above the swampy marsh. Just their simple existence is contingent on the natural environment, an inescapable fact no

OPPOSITE: *Afton Villa in Saint Francisville, Louisiana*

matter how many colorful impatiens or hibiscus or camellias are imported.

In New Orleans proper there are several notable gardens. Longue Vue is singled out for several reasons, not the least of which is the artistic hand of Ellen Biddle Shipman, one of the twentieth century's most important landscape architects. Spanish Court is always mentioned, and it is remarkable to see how the Islamic aesthetics of the Generalife Gardens in Granada, Spain, are translated into this southern milieu. But there are many other things taking place at Longue Vue, and garden enthusiasts should approach it with careful attention. Within a pleasant drive from New Orleans is an entirely different kind of garden. Crosby Arboretum makes a case for being the most important ecological garden in the country. After more than twenty years it is truly a tremendous place, with the evidence of natural succession taking hold in mysterious, enthralling ways. In particular the pine savannah is an eloquent statement, as articulate and wonderful a piece of art as any great painting or sculpture.

Although a bit off the beaten path, the Arkansas gardens are worthy places. Eureka Springs Gardens are located within the dramatic landscape of the Ozarks, a natural eden that is fast disappearing as casinos and other aspects of tourism quickly take hold here.

DELTA REGION: ARKANSAS

1 Eureka Springs: Eureka Springs Gardens

LOCATION: OFF U. S. ROUTE 62, FIVE-AND-HALF MILES WEST OF EUREKA SPRINGS CITY LIMITS

GARDEN OPEN: 9 am to 6 pm daily, May–October, 9 am to 5 pm daily, November and April; closed December–March.
ADMISSION: $6.45 adults.

FURTHER INFORMATION FROM: Rt. 6, Box 362, Eureka Springs 72632
(501) 253-9244
www.eurekagardens.com

NEARBY SIGHTS OF INTEREST: Thorncrown Chapel, Onyx Cave, Pea Ridge Battlefield

The natural beauty of the Ozark Mountains reaches an epiphany at Eureka Springs, a craggy little town known for its pure spring water. The town's gardens, which were developed in 1993 and have progressed at breakneck pace, border the Blue Spring, a 500-foot-deep hole from which chilly Mediterranean blue water erupts and flows by lagoon to the White River, Blue Spring forms an elegant spine to a display of richly colored annuals and shrubs. A meadow nearby has been converted into an idea garden, with mulch paths delineating residential-scale flower beds containing suggestions for the home gardeners. At the far end of the property, occupying a little wooded knoll, is one of the most artful woodland gardens, with a narrow, gently sloping (handicapped accessible) path climbing a series of rock outcroppings. Oaks, pawpaw, and other native trees encompass the whole scene. The rock is highlighted in various places by accents of color (mainly bulbs) in a soft, sophisticated manner. There's even a garden area dedicated to President and Mrs. Clinton, featuring an abstract limestone sculpture with the plantings supposedly reflecting favorites of this First Lady.

A layered canvas treads the line between artifice and natural at Eureka Springs.

DELTA REGION: ARKANSAS

garden open: dawn to dusk daily, year-round. ADMISSION: $6 garden tour, $10 boat ride on Lake Hamilton.

FURTHER INFORMATION FROM:
Department of Landscape Architecture
230 Memorial Hall,
Fayetteville 72701
(888) 530-6873

NEARBY SIGHTS OF INTEREST:
Hot Springs National Park

A tree peony in the Garvan Woodland

2 Hot Springs: Garvan Woodland Gardens

LOCATION: JUST SOUTH OF THE INTERSECTION OF THE INTERSTATE 270 BYPASS AND STATE ROUTE 128, OFF ARKRIDGE ROAD, ON THE EAST SIDE OF LAKE HAMILTON

This garden, formerly called the Twentieth Century Gardens, is located on a 210-acre tract of unspoiled woodland. The property was originally purchased by local businessman Arthur B. Cook for its timber prospects, but his daughter, Verna Garvan, succeeded in preserving it instead, eventually bequeathing it to the University of Arkansas Landscape Architecture Program in 1985. Several different garden walks have been designed within the existing canopy of hickory, sweet gum, and oaks. These include a hill of daffodils, featuring an overly large selection of blue varieties that enliven the normal hot colors. A handsome stone walkway cuts through the garden, while a teak bench designed by Mrs. Garvan provides a place to rest and meditate on the springtime glory of the space. At one time a local brick industry used part of this property, and what remains has been fashioned into a garden. The old red bricks are encircled by flower borders and shrubs to create an unusual, russet rock garden. The university's curator has continued Garvan's thirty years' of work to integrate gardenesque designs into the natural landscape, taking formal elements, such as heritage roses, and arranging them in naturalistic displays—as walks, carpets, and pathways. In the center of the garden is a pavilion designed by architect Fay Jones. It is a magnificent work, built with solid wood beams and glass, that soars from the woods.

DELTA REGION: MISSISSIPPI

3 Jackson: Mynelle Gardens

LOCATION: CORNER OF CLINTON BOULEVARD AND COUNTRY CLUB ROAD, JUST OFF INTERSTATE 220.

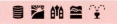

GARDEN OPEN: 9:00 am to 5:15 pm daily, March–October, 8:00 am to 4:15 pm daily, November–February.
ADMISSION: $2.00 adults, $0.50 children.

FURTHER INFORMATION FROM: 4736 Clinton Boulevard, Jackson 39209
(601) 960-1894

NEARBY SIGHTS OF INTEREST: Smith-Robertson Museum, Manship House

These lovely city gardens were originally planted by an enterprising woman named Mynelle Westerbrook Green. Mynelle came to this little corner of Jackson when her parents built the antebellum-style house onsite. It was originally surrounded by a small courtyard garden, but Mynelle was more interested in large display gardens of perennials that she transformed into a small business: Greenbrook Flowers. The business continues to thrive, but in the 1940s Mynelle left it to her daughter and moved to Illinois. When she and her husband returned to Jackson in the 1950s the old flower gardens had been neglected. Through the decade she worked tirelessly to restore them, far exceeding her original work. Since she did not have the imperative of business to concern her, the modern landscape became a varied display of designed gardens. In the middle of the garden is a fish pond, which Mynelle took pains to form into an undulating, romantic water feature. In the middle of the pond, connected by walking bridges, sits a small island that is planted with Japanese maples, dwarf conifers, and rock outcroppings in an Asian style. The far reaches of the garden become more naturalistic and more parklike, with a large greensward framed by white gardens and an extensive area of naturalized irises. Mynelle also imported a tremendous number of azaleas and camellias, which do quite well in this climate. The presentation is largely done within a woodland environment where the dappled light allows the colors of these normally vibrant plants to intensify. By the time she was finished friends were calling this magnificent creation "Mynelle Gardens," and in 1953, sated at last, this intrepid gardener deeded the property to the city.

Mynelle's life's work, lovingly transformed

DELTA REGION: MISSISSIPPI

DELTA REGION: MISSISSIPPI

4 Picayune: Crosby Arboretum

LOCATION: EXIT 4 ON INTERSTATE 59, ADJACENT TO THE MISSISSIPPI WELCOME CENTER

GARDEN OPEN: 9 am to 5 pm Wednesday–Sunday, year-round except major holidays.
ADMISSION: $4 adults, $2 children.

FURTHER INFORMATION FROM:
370 Ridge Road, Picayune 39466
(601) 799-2311

NEARBY SIGHTS OF INTEREST: NASA Space Center, Bogue Chitto National Wildlife Refuge

As Faulkner reminds us, Mississippi has, in many ways, always been a kind of forgotten place. Travel publications tell us about New Orleans, the hills of Georgia, but not about the hardwood and wetlands of Mississippi. The state has remained a mystery in more ways than one—for example, until recently there was no list of what kinds of plants grew there. This changed in 1981 when a group of landscape and ecology enthusiasts at Mississippi State University banded together to create the first regional arboretum in this part of the South. Armed with seed money from the descendents of L. O. Crosby, a local forester and philanthropist, the group set out to create a showcase for the native landscape of the Mississippi lowlands. One problem stood in their way. What were the native plants?

The problem was caused by more than academic neglect or the simple fact that no botanist had taken the time to catalogue thoroughly the flora of the state. It stemmed, as well, from the fact that the landscape of Mississippi has been altered so completely over the last 150 years that today there exist many types of plants that may be considered "native." For millenia the landscape of Mississippi was ravaged by wildfires, which promoted the development of a superabundant pine savannah—essential partly sunny meadows dotted with large pine trees. But in the nineteenth and early twentieth centuries, these lands were extensively forested, and quick cash crops were planted. Since the 1940s much of that agricultural land has been returned to natural woodland, but with the important caveat of modern fire control. The result is a new landscape of lowland hardwoods.

Crosby Arboretum makes the unique assertion that each of these landscapes is important and valuable. The site lies within the Pearl River basin and a series of streams, ponds, wetlands, and bogs occupies the center. Arranged on either side of the wetlands are the new woodland landscape and the precontact *Piney*. The woodlands are carefully managed to encourage the health of the ecosystem and natural succession, which (in simplistic terms) is the prolonged evolution of a forest from immature conifers to mature deciduous. The process has been underway from almost twenty years, and the results are prodigious, with a climax beech–magnolia forest coming into its own on the western portions of the site. The savannah has

OPPOSITE: *A light morning mist coats the savannah.*

BELOW: *Fay Jones' pavilion, Pinecote, draws inspiration from the natural beauty of the Mississippi lowlands.*

been regularly burned to create a series of garden rooms. Each features a different plant association, with the general tenor being a verdant carpet of wildflower meadow—excitingly red or yellow, depending on the year and climatic conditions—punctuated with pines, the trunks of which form a kind of rhythm across the land.

The genius of the arboretum is how carefully planned and controlled it is, and how little this shows. The entire landscape is designed as a painstakingly quilted fabric of one landscape type giving over to another. Since we're talking nature here, and not architecture, this is accomplished by creating a kind of structure and then letting natural processes run their course against it. For instance, in order to segregate the savannah a vocabulary of wetland edges was developed. These are thin, linear depressions that hold water and wet plants, such as gum trees and reeds, which prevent the fires that burn the savannah from affecting the woodland (and thus converting it to savannah). The result of these artificial interventions is that the entire garden becomes a kind compressed version of the entire state of Mississippi.

The experience of the arboretum takes place along a matrix of trails. The entrance trail, a short walk from the parking lot to the visitor center, is perhaps the most thrilling, for it cuts across all three landscape types in rapid succession, giving one a head-spinning introduction to the intense diversity of sights, sounds, and textures to be found here. Once inside, there are three separate walks each focusing on a type. Along the way are well-designed interpretive kiosks that describe both the flora and fauna as well as the ecological processes (as best we understand them) that allow it all to take place. At the center, both spiritually and structurally, of the arboretum is Pinecote, a pavilion designed by E. Fay Jones. Jones was part of the original design team for the arboretum (which also included landscape architect Edward Blake) and expressed the profound beauty of the site in this stunning work. It is a simple, open building, with a treelike branching of pine columns and beams that seem to blend into the woodlands surrounding it. On one face the structure opens up to a pond, over which it seems to hover. And at night, when the A-frame roof is light from below, it shimmers.

Jones' pavilion won the American Institute of Architects honor award, while the arboretum took the same commendation from the American Society of Landscape Architects. Both awards symbolize the importance of this tremendous garden, which in twenty short years has become perhaps the single best expression of southern landscape in the region.

TOP: *Pitcher plants fill the wet fields.*

MIDDLE: *Annual burning of the savannah reduces undergrowth and refreshes the ecosystem.*

BOTTOM: *A light morning mist coats the savannah.*

5 Shreveport: American Rose Center

LOCATION: EXIT 5 ON I-20

Roses are perhaps the most beloved flower in America, although lately there has been much disdain aired about their high maintenance. Nonetheless when a new botanical garden gets off the ground inevitably some "rosarian" lobbies for a rose garden. Shreveport is the mecca of roses, for this is where the venerable American Rose Society finally took root in the 1950s. The actual organization is over a hundred years old, but it has had several homes. Here, however, it has made great strides, and set up a wonderful clearinghouse for information about all the varieties of roses. There are 118 acres of roses arranged as 60 different gardens. Most are test beds, but the displays can also be magical, with some formal areas, some informal areas, and in some cases just fields and fields of roses. Data comes into the center from 24 all-America selection sites around the country; information is digested and disseminated to 24,000 members. In this horticultural capital it is easy to see why roses are called "America's floral emblem," for no matter how much certain trends catch on it's hard to believe there could ever be as much time, energy, and infrastructure invested in any other individual plant. It makes environmentalists, who object to the pesticide use and unsustainability of modern roses, cringe. Yet the stakes here extend beyond ecology. The rose, in many ways, is more than a plant. It has become a symbol—romantic, sentimental, and historic, which reminds us of simpler times.

GARDEN OPEN: dawn to dusk Monday–Friday. ADMISION: free.

FURTHER INFORMATION FROM:
8877 Jefferson-Paige Road, Shreveport 71119
(318) 938-5402
www.ars.org

NEARBY SIGHTS OF INTEREST:
Norton Art Gallery

A few of the 60 different rose gardens

GARDEN OPEN: dawn to dusk daily. **ADMISSION:** free.

FURTHER INFORMATION FROM:
U.S. 171, Many 71449
(800) 354-3523

NEARBY SIGHTS OF INTEREST:
Block House Church

An old garden off the beaten track has matured gracefully.

6 Many: Hodges Garden

LOCATION: U. S. ROUTE 171 BETWEEN MANY AND LEESVILLE

This garden is integrated into a public park, and in fact provides much of the floral infrastructure for the landscape. There are no formal garden areas other than a conservatory, rather the collections are woven into a natural park fabric of woodlands and greensward. In the springtime there is an excellent display of naturalized bulb and perennial borders that accent walkways. Daffodils and tulips predominate, igniting the ground plane beneath a verdant canopy of magnolia and sweet olive. There are also hundreds of azaleas, some of which are enclosed in the woods and some of which are left in the open. In the summer the scene changes to the hotter presence of hydrangeas and crepe myrtle. In the greenhouse there is an ample display of bromeliads and orchids, enhanced by an ever-changing exhibit of palms, succulents, and other tropicals.

GARDEN OPEN: 9:00 am to 4:30 pm daily, March–June and October–November.
ADMISSION: $5.

FURTHER INFORMATION FROM:
P.O. Box 993, Saint Francisville 70775
(504) 635-6330

NEARBY SIGHTS OF INTEREST:
Rosedown Plantation, The Myrtles, Saint Francisville

7 Saint Francisville: Afton Villa

LOCATION: JUST NORTH OF SAINT FRANCISVILLE ON U. S. ROUTE 61, THIRTY-FIVE MILES NORTH OF BATON ROUGE

Afton Villa is an anomaly in the world of historic preservation. Usually historic gardens are an accouterment to a historic house, restored only as an afterthought to the architecture. But at this property such protocols have been reversed. In 1963 the Gothic manor house (originally built in the 1850s) burned to the ground, and ten years later when the property was subsequently rescued by the philanthropically minded Morrell and Genevieve Trimble, it was the garden that claimed their attentions and not the house. To all appearances the entry drive bespeaks a typical antebellum estate: ancient live oaks form a low canopy that subdues the Louisiana sun; on the dirt road one seems to amble at the road's pace, and the silver strands of

Spanish moss contrast artfully with the brilliance of a collection of venerable azaleas, some of which are over a hundred years old while others are of a variety unique to the garden called Afton reds. The eye expects to see a grand old mansion rise around the next bend, but when we get to the circular parking area what we find are an old brick terrace, four marble statues, and the knee-high ruins of what once must have been a glorious southern home. The gardens are stitched into the fabric of these ruins, using the architecture as a tableau for a display that is multilayered and complex. There is plenty of show here: hundreds of daffodils and other perennials that explode through the spring. Yet perhaps because of their condensed scale, or maybe owing to the delicate hand and restrained taste of their proprietors, the gardens have a subtle effect that can leave one wandering for hours in complete wonder.

In the late 1970s the Trimbles hired Neil Oldenwald, director of the landscape architecture school at Louisiana State University, to "renew" the garden. Strictly speaking what we find today is not a restoration; most of the design is a contemporary undertaking that reflects Genevieve Trimble's tastes and inclinations. The *Ruins Gardens* are completely new. Here Oldenwald and Trimble combined a varied plant palette of climbing vines, hedge, and flowers in thin quantities that weave through the brick and mortar foundation of the house. Half walls still stand in some places and are adorned with an assortment of potted flowers. During the seasons the coloring evolves through the hot shades, all the while retaining a kind of delicate presence and never becoming overbearing. Below the house lie the original formal gardens, which are more strictly structured. Centered around a central, moss-covered brick plaza lie four beds outlined in boxwood and filled with a profusion of color-coded flowers. The rich architectural vocabulary, including a sundial resting on a marble base in the center of the plaza and an iron bench placed on an overlook at one end, are carefully situated to provide focal points and viewing positions to optimize the experience. Rather than wander, one looks.

The precise opposite is true of the next room in the garden, what is called the *Parterre Garden*. Here an overgrown tumble of boxwood and azalea are planted in a tight maze. A collection of sturdy camellias and sweet olive complete the scene, while a sin-

TOP: *The parterre gardens reflect the landscape as it used to be.*

BOTTOM: *. . . including the music room, where statuary of the muses sits in a grove.*

gle incredible live oak overhangs the entire area, casting much appreciated shade. In the center of this room lies the original Afton azalea, from which all the others were propagated beginning in 1900. The property slopes off from these terraces toward a ravine. Oldenwald restored the *Grand Staircase* of grass terraces that reaches down toward a shade garden located next to the stream.

Several other garden rooms fill out the forty acres of managed lands at Afton Villa, some of which are of a more contemporary nature, including the *Daffodil Valley* where the Trimbles have experimented with different varieties in a naturalistic setting. The best time to visit is in the morning during the week when the only soul around is the gatekeeper, an amiable fellow who cheerily passes along the self-guided walking tour. The rest is what you make of it.

8 Baton Rouge: Hilltop Arboretum

GARDEN OPEN: dawn to dusk daily, year-round. **ADMISSION:** free.

FURTHER INFORMATION FROM:
P.O. Box 82608, Baton Rouge 70884
(504) 767-6916
www.hilltop.lsu.edu

NEARBY SIGHTS OF INTEREST:
Rural Life Museum, Maritime Museum

LOCATION: HIGHLAND ROAD, FOUR MILES SOUTH OF LOUISIANA STATE UNIVERSITY; NORTH OF THE INTERSTATE 10 EXIT

Hilltop was the country home of Emory Smith, a connoisseur of native flora, who donated the property to Louisiana State University in 1991. A stroll through Smith's Hilltop property today gives one the feeling of being in Louisiana more than anywhere else. The ancient live oaks on the property are simply magnificent, while the varied topography of eroded gorges and rising hillocks give the sense of entering a magical land. Of particular note in this landscape garden is the green room, achieved by neatly trimming back the canopy and carving out an intimate, completely secluded nook.

A slight ravine adds depth and structure to the layered forest of Louisiana.

9. New Orleans: New Orleans Botanical Garden

LOCATION: WISNER AVENUE AND INTERSTATE 610, DOWNTOWN

The New Orleans Botanical Garden was built as a city rose garden in the 1930s by the Works Progress Administration, with wonderful Art Deco touches in the gazebos and a classical layout. The garden, originally executed by landscape architect William Wiedorn, has grown up over the years and is well-maintained by the city parks department. The rose garden has been added to many times during garden's sixty-year life and remains the central attraction. It consists of several pavilions and beds lined with hedge. There are also several architectural features, such as romantic statuary and a sundial. Stitched around this is the venerable collection of roses. The conservatory collections of bromeliads, ferns, and orchids wrap around a lily pond and several pieces of romantic sculpture. A unique WPA footprint is found in the cold frames and horticultural trial beds. This is where all the plant material for the parks department was grown for many years; today the area is used as a testing facility. The old potting shed has been converted into a garden study center, adorned with a small butterfly garden.

GARDEN OPEN: 10:00 am to 4:30 pm Tuesday–Sunday.
ADMISSION: $3 adults, $1 children.

FURTHER INFORMATION FROM:
1 Palm Drive, New Orleans 70124
(504) 483-9386

NEARBY SIGHTS OF INTEREST:
Fairgrounds, French Quarter

A city garden captures the romantic essence of New Orleans.

DELTA REGION: LOUISIANA

LONGUE VUE HOUSE
EAST LAWN
SPANISH COURT
VISITOR PARKING
COURT
OFFICE SHOP
ENTRANCE COURT
DISCOVERY GARDEN
WILD GARDEN

10 New Orleans: Longue Vue House and Gardens

LOCATION: OFF METARIE ROAD (INTERSTATE 10 EXIT 231A), TEN MINUTES WEST OF DOWNTOWN

GARDEN OPEN: 10:00 am to 4:30 pm Monday–Saturday, 1:00 pm to 5:00 pm Sunday, year-round. **ADMISSION:** $7 adults, $3 children.

FURTHER INFORMATION FROM:
7 Bamboo Road, New Orleans 70124
(508) 488-5488
www.longuevue.com

NEARBY SIGHTS OF INTEREST:
New Orleans Garden District

The splendid, small water garden is inspired by Islamic influences.

Most visitors mistake Longue Vue for an antebellum plantation that somehow has survived the years. The effect of the enormous live oaks along the formal entry drive, the handsome brick walls that line the perimeter of the property, and the neoclassical architecture all give this impression. But actually Longue Vue is a twentieth-century place—distinct in its restrained taste and modern in its cosmopolitan outlook.

Longue Vue was begun in 1921 when Edith Rosenwald (of the Sears Roebuck empire) and Edgar Stern purchased a small piece of property on the edge of the New Orleans Country Club. After about twenty years they tired of the original Georgian house and hired architects William and Geoffrey Platt to construct a smaller, tastefully neoclassical manor in 1942. According to history books one reason they remodeled was that the first house had too few windows through which to view the wonderful gardens. These were designed, beginning in 1935, largely by Ellen Biddle Shipman, a rising landscape architect from the northeast whom Edith Stern called "the godmother of the house." Shipman was also called in to execute the interior design of the house, and one of the great stories of the estate is how closely connected the inside and outside spaces feel. As we walk around the immediate boundary of the house we see this in three distinct garden spaces. The *Pan Garden* is located off the dining room. This is an intimate viewing garden that takes a statue of this mischievous deity as its focal point. Hemmed in by squat versions of the dark brick walls that are ubiquitous around the property, the garden responds with blue and purple hues to create a rich, lush feeling. The interior space is so conformed that the windows seem narrowed down on the space, focused on a minute space—the state of Pan perhaps, or maybe the stonework—for the sake of everything else. Off the other side of the house, the *Yellow Garden* designed by Mrs. Stern provides the antithesis of this idea. Obviously

DELTA REGION: LOUISIANA

Looking over an old wall to see the house through the garden

OPPOSITE, TOP: *Details, such as this mosaic tile work, are replicated from the Generalife in Spain.*

MIDDLE: *A classic arbor frames the space.*

BOTTOM: *Looking out to the upper and lower gardens from the porch*

yellow overwhelms the garden but the counterpoint is more complex than this. As much as the darker garden is inwardly focused, this space is outwardly oriented. From the small terrace cupped against the house there are several sharply framed vistas across the grounds. Several comfortable chairs set about allow prolonged enjoyment and study. In the center of the space sits a fountain containing a sculptural work of three dolphins leaping in a faintly abstracted arc. It is the work of contemporary artist Lyn Emery.

The *Portico Garden,* which sits at the center of Longue Vue, is a rich formal parterre garden featuring a splendid collection of camellias. It dates back to 1935 and has been well tended over the years. A central axis leads from the intimate, enclosed spaces close to the house out into the sun, while the parterres are evenly balanced in quarters, with wisps of flowers barely climbing over them. After dropping off the terrace, the landscape opens farther into a great lawn, which Shipman called the *Spanish Court*. Originally designed as an extension of the Portico Garden by Shipman, this garden was destroyed by a hurricane in 1965. Architect William Platt collaborated with Stern on a redesign, which is based upon a close study of the great Generalife Islamic gardens at the Alhambra in Granada, Spain. A central greensward, flat as a sheet of steel, flows through the rectangular space, flanked on either side by low-lying cisterns of water. An intimate, noble feeling is cast by the handsome brick walls that are covered in ivy and march alongside the lawn in stately fashion. The axis of the Portico Garden is revived in a narrow stone canal equipped with dancing water jets. It, and the entire space at large, finally culminates in a semicircular pool surrounded by a loggia and potted plants. The space is not a literal replication of the Generalife. Those gardens actually occupy a great mountainside near the center of Granada, and use a complex, ancient system of pools and runnels to power the fountains (of which there are several) by gravity alone. These fountains, lying in a completely flat lowland, are powered electrically. The aesthetic, of course, also responds to local conditions. The surrounding woods of live oaks, magnolias, and sweet olive are permanent fixtures that interact with the design. The greensward and walled enclosure have a warm southern feeling rather than the desert character of their Mediterranean inspiration. And yet on a very ephemeral level there are commonalties. Both spaces—this in smaller form—

lift the spirit with classic, noble lines, and teach us something about the gracefulness of sharp form.

Lying behind the Spanish Court, as if in hiding, is the *Pond Garden*, a little space cupped by the far extent of the property. There are Asian influences here, particularly in the idea that it should be seen from the single viewing place. But Shipman's planting design is more akin to the picturesque rambles of classic English estates. Hostas, water lilies, and an ornate mesh of woody shrubs create a diverse canvas for a light smattering of bloomage in the spring. On the other side of the Spanish Court, arranged in a circuit around the edge of the property, are several other garden areas. The first is the Walled Garden. Set into the woods, this is a secretive square space of classically carved flower beds all trained upon a central fountain. The whole planting scheme has been restored, so the area looks a little wan. The same is true for what promises someday to be one of the most beautiful parts of Longue Vue: the Wild Garden. At this point, it is simply a short circuit of walkways winding through native shrubs. But as the area grows up around these "bones" it will provide an important counterpoint to the surrounding suburban encroachment. Longue Vue has also created a new children's garden, designed by the local firm Design Consortium. While often such an addition would insert a gaudy, loud, and hence inappropriate element into an otherwise sophisticated place, the execution here works. Educational art pieces structure the garden, and yet are formed to be inherently interesting. A historic greenhouse was left during construction and now forms a teaching classroom. But the most wonderful part is the dark secret garden occupying a forgotten corner where a tapestry of palmettos is pulled back to reveal a quiet, dark little nook. Its purpose, obviously, is to teach lessons about natural spaces that fall beyond the purview of biology books.

Winding back around to tour the gardens again (which must be done!) we catch the wonderful southern entry, with enormous live oaks framing the house and panels edged in mondo grass providing a viewing plinth. It is a classic scene, fit for any movie or novel, or even just for a garden experience that epitomizes the south.

The restored garden retains Ellen Biddle Shipman's original touches.

11 New Orleans: Garden District

LOCATION: DOWNTOWN NEW ORLEANS

Every city has its prettiest residential areas, places in the urban fabric where people take a little more pride in their surroundings. In New Orleans this has gained full expression in a little neighborhood on the southwest side of town. The Garden District is not a public garden in the sense that these are all private residential gardens; entry by the general public is prohibited and gardens can viewed from the public sidewalk alone. But you can see them from beyond the fence line, and a morning's stroll through the neighborhood can give you (and other passersby you will meet) a good taste of the gardens—southern gardening at its finest. Each house has a different character and yet a common palette and shared spirit bind the small landscapes together.

GARDENS OPEN: dawn to dusk daily. **ADMISSION:** free (please respect the privacy of individual homeowners).

NEARBY SIGHTS OF INTEREST: Audubon Zoo

The Garden District provides a voyeuristic glimpse of Louisiana society.

DELTA REGION: LOUISIANA

12 Avery Island: Jungle Gardens

GARDEN OPEN: dawn to dusk daily. **ADMISSION:** $5.75 adult, $4.00 children.

FURTHER INFORMATION:
General Delivery, Avery Island 70513
(318) 369-6243
www.tabasco.com

NEARBY SIGHTS OF INTEREST:
Petit Paris Museum, Live Oak Gardens

LOCATION: U. S. ROUTE 90 SOUTH FROM LAFAYETTE, TO STATE ROUTE 14, TO THE END OF STATE ROUTE 329; 70 MILES NORTHWEST OF HOUMA

Avery Island is home to Tabasco sauce inventor and entrepreneur E. A. McIlhenny's vast empire, including fields of red chilies that extend to the horizon and a vast 200-acre nature preserve called Jungle Gardens. McIlhenny, or "Monsieur Ned" as his friends knew him, was a consummate conservationist. In 1895, when the snowy egret was on the verge of extinction, McIlhenny built a small aviary on his island, which today is a massively populated "bird world." The Jungle Gardens are actually an incredibly verdant patch of humus lying atop a massive salt dome that extends almost eight miles beneath the earth's surface. (Salt, of course, is one of the main ingredients in Tabasco; pepper is the other—which prompts the company to tout that Avery Island is where salt and pepper first met.) Anchoring the gardens is the native landscape of live oaks, many of which are hundreds of years old. Into this, McIlhenny and his descendents have woven a complex admixture of exotic plants brought from all over the world. There are pools of lotus and papyrus from the upper Nile, Chinese wisteria growing into an arch over a reflective pool, and plenty of bamboo. But most of all you'll see thousands of azaleas and camellias, with which McIlhenny had a profound romance. Many curios dot the landscape as well, chief of which is the Buddhist temple featuring a Chinese statue dating from the tenth century. The place still makes Tabasco sauce and still maintains the gardens in exceptional condition, with an eye for local beauty and whatever's quirky and cool.

The "inscrutable Gautama," a tenth-century Buddha in the middle of an exotic bayou landscape.

13 New Iberia: Rip Van Winkle Gardens

LOCATION: JEFFERSON ISLAND, OFF STATE ROUTE 14, WEST OF NEW IBERIA

GARDEN OPEN: 9 am to 5 pm daily, year-round. **ADMISSION:** $9.00 adults, $8.50 seniors, $7.00 youth, $5.00 children.

FURTHER INFORMATION FROM: 5505 Rip Van Winkle Road, New Iberia 70560 (318) 365-3332 www.ripvanwinkle.com

NEARBY SIGHTS OF INTEREST: Avery Island, Acadian Village

The southern coast of Louisiana is dotted with salt domes from a vast bed six miles below the surface. These "fingers" or "domes" push the soil up above the normally flat and swamp-covered landscape to create verdant uplands of hardwoods—predominately composed of live oaks. These are perfect places for gardens, as E. A. McIlhenny discovered at Avery Island, and as Joseph Jefferson discovered on his land. Jefferson, a famous stage actor during the mid-nineteenth century, owned several properties in New England, New Jersey, and here. Jefferson built the large southern mansion on the property and laid out the grounds in an English manner, meaning he used curving roads and the natural topography to create an experience of the landscape. This is particularly evident in the entry drive that parts through a stately grove of ancient live oaks. In the 1910s the property was purchased by salt prospector J. Lyle Bayless Sr., and his son (J. Lyle Jr.) set about designing wonderful floral gardens. Bayless worked with an English horticulturist, Geoffrey Wakefield, and imported thousands of plants, including an incredible collection of camellias, which they soon were grafting themselves. In the 1960s the gardens were named *Rip Van Winkle Gardens,* after the character that Joseph Jefferson had made famous on stage a century earlier and opened to the public. But disaster struck in the 1980s when an oil drilling operation broke through the salt dome under the lake. Within seven hours several billion gallons of water, along with several barges and Bayless' new lake house, vanished into a great muddy hole. Then a large circle of land sank precipitously, destroying almost fifty acres of gardens. Bayless was crushed and moved to Hawaii, but the local foundation to which he sold the gardens to set about restoring them. On one hand it's hard to imagine that today's gardens are as great as the original, considering the magnitude of damage. But on the other, what we see today is so breathtaking that one quickly loses sight that there could ever have been anything better. The reason why the gardens have survived is undoubtedly the wealth of live oak trees. (The garden was renamed the Live Oak Gardens for several years, but recently reverted back to its original name when sold to new owners.) Against this backdrop are several individual gardens, including a small herb garden, a formal bedded-out annual garden, and a Japanese-style garden. Camellias are still a major attraction, while the versatile staff has infused the gardens with a greater variety of plants.

The expansive landscape of classic live oaks has withstood natural traumas.

1. Tallahassee: Alfred B. Maclay State Gardens
2. Orlando: Harry P. Leu Gardens
3. Kissimmee: World of Orchids
4. Winter Haven: Cypress Gardens
5. Lake Wales: Bok Tower Gardens
6. Sarasota: Marie Selby Botanical Gardens
7. Fort Myers: Edison Estate
8. Fort Pierce: Heathcote Botanical Gardens
9. West Palm Beach: Mounts Botanical Garden
10. Fort Lauderdale: Flamingo Gardens
11. Miami: Vizcaya
12. Miami: Fairchild Tropical Garden
13. Key West: Nancy Forrestor's Secret Garden
14. Key West: Audubon House

FLORIDA

Florida is really like two states—or maybe even three. The regions in north Florida are more akin to the gardens of Georgia and Alabama than to the southern part of the state. The palette of the Maclay Gardens—pine needle paths, camellias, live oaks—is a good example. Likewise, as one moves deeper into the tropical regions of south Florida, one seems to be moving almost into a new country. Orange groves and naturalized palms are indicators of a deeper shift. Attitudes toward gardens are different in the far south of Florida. We find here a number of gardens that are actual businesses, that formed themselves not with university grants or public donations, but upon the basic economic principle that people will pay to see something strange. This *something strange* here, of course, is the Florida landscape itself, with its otherworldly jungles where anything and everything seems to grow.

In Miami the measure of gardening is made against the Fairchild Tropical Garden, named after a famous plant explorer. It has evolved into one of the most significant general collections of tropical plants in the country. On a more specialized level, there is the World of Orchids, a nursery-turned-garden near Disney World, and the Marie Selby Gardens, an old Saratoga estate that has evolved into a living laboratory for epiphytes (Spanish moss). All of these are serious research institutions as well as public education gardens. While botanica is a major theme in the state, there are several designed gardens that take a more traditionally artistic approach. Chief among these are the rococo gardens at Vizcaya, a bric-a-brac estate on the bay south of Miami that was assembled from pieces of European manor houses salvaged after World War II. In some ways these gardens are too much. And yet their exquisiteness is so intense that they are given extra treatment here.

Gardens have always been political, and one of today's great battles is taking place in Key West. The issue is sprawl and

OPPOSITE: *Cypress Gardens river boat*

the disappearance of not only open, natural space but the traditional, bohemian variety that has characterized the island for so many years. Nancy Forrester's Secret Garden is one of the last honest places on Key West. A small, eclectic space of wild tropical plants, it represents a true radicalism in a sea of encroaching condominiums and time shares.

Heathcote Botanical Gardens in Fort Pierce, Florida

Tallahassee: Alfred B. Maclay State Gardens

LOCATION: ONE MILE NORTH OF INTERSTATE 10 (EXIT 30), ON U.S. ROUTE 319

Alfred B. Maclay was a New York financier who purchased this lakeside property with his wife, Louise Fleischman, in 1923. Maclay had a particular affinity for landscape, and over a twenty-year period he set about creating a wonderfully subtle green garden with just the right amount of color during the winter-blooming months. In place of tropicals, the garden is composed of the underlying structure of oaks and pines, and accentuated with dogwoods, azaleas, and camellias. The visit is organized as a series of walks, beginning with the house. Here Mrs. Maclay, who took over tending the grounds after her husband's death in 1944, created a sunny, open space, defined along its edges by a deeply layered fabric of greenery, composed mostly of dogwood and redbud set against the architecture of some stately old live oaks. Note in the ground plane the use of arrowroot (here called coontie), a spiney-leaf shrub traditionally used in bread making. A walk through a diverse gathering of camellias forms the second major space in the garden. Many of the individual plants are quite old, with some dating over a century. A brick walled garden concludes the walk. This is the most formal space in the landscape, and features a closely cropped lawn carpet split into terraces by thin wisps of stone. A reflecting pool framed by stairs and clay pots anchors the space and provides a viewing platform for a vista of Lake Hall through an arched gate. Wooded walkways of grass lined by thin scrims of azaleas, an oblong pond ringed with reeds and mondo grass, and a pine needle path defined by anise and viburnum—a unique and aesthetically pleasing combination of contrasting textures—round out the various rooms of the garden. In 1953 Louise Maclay donated the gardens to the state, and today it is maintained as a state park, adjoining a recreational preserve and the lake. The garden continues to be maintained in the style to which it had become accustomed, exuding a richness of character all too unusual in the modern world.

GARDEN OPEN: 9 am to dusk daily. ADMISSION, January–March: $3.00 adults, $1.50 children.

FURTHER INFORMATION FROM:
3540 Thomasville Road,
Tallahassee 32308
(904) 487-4115

NEARBY SIGHTS OF INTEREST:
Natural Bridge Battlefield

Despite the discouraging sign, an attractive garden at the estate of Alfred Maclay.

FLORIDA

GARDEN OPEN: 9 am to 5 pm daily, year-round. **ADMISSION:** modest fee.

FURTHER INFORMATION FROM: 1920 North Forest Avenue, Orlando 32803-1537
(407) 246-2620

NEARBY SIGHTS OF INTEREST: Planetarium, Gatorland Zoo

Roses envelop one of the many romantic spaces at the Leu Gardens.

2 Orlando: Harry P. Leu Gardens

LOCATION: FOREST AVENUE AND CORRINE DRIVE, OFF STATE ROUTE 50, TEN MILES NORTH OF DOWNTOWN ORLANDO

Henry Leu probably had his eye on the big old house on North Forest Avenue most of his life, and when ambition and luck combined in his business pursuits in the 1930s he finally purchased it. The home was originally built in 1888 and completed several owners later in 1906. Impressive as the house is, Leu's great contribution was to the garden, which he planted with a world-class collection of camellias as well as exotics gathered from world travels. The property was formed into a museum and the garden designated as a botanical garden in 1961. Since then it has grown and been augmented considerably. Several formal gardens lie close to the house. The rose garden is a typical geometrical layout, with a gazebo at its center, four axial paths, and over a thousand different plants. Immediately adjacent to this, and lying just a step away from the house, are test plots for annuals, planted amid an airy woodland setting of oaks. A path takes visitors deeper into the woods, which with its stately mature canopy and well-tended collection of hardwoods, may be the garden's greatest attribute. Within the forest are Leu's abundant collection of camellias, palms, bamboo, and cycads, all of which are being tested for hardiness. Lake Rowena provides a backdrop and anchor for the gardens, and at its crook is a wooden boardwalk through a quiet native wetland garden harboring a diversity of wildlife, including various colorful birds and the occasional alligator. Nearby lies the Ravine Garden where a feeder creek to the lake forms a spine for a vertically arranged presentation of banana, ginger, tree ferns, and other tropicals. A white room, a native plants collection, a garden of hibiscus, and various other small, smartly designed areas complete this diverse and thoughtful place, which, considering the theme-park context of the area, is a respite from the hubbub.

3 Kissimmee: World of Orchids

LOCATION: EXIT 25B ON INTERSTATE 4, TWO MILES WEST ON U. S. ROUTE 192, THEN ONE MILE SOUTH ON STATE ROUTE 545.

The World of Orchids developed from nursery growers Kerry and Christiana Richards' worst fears. Until 1993 the Richards grew and sold world-class orchids in south Florida. But worried about the increasingly danger of hurricanes, the couple decided to move farther north, to a piece of property in Kissimmee. Just before the move date, Hurricane Andrew destroyed much of their Miami nursery. Luckily enough stock survived—both in terms of actual flowers and growers' spirit—and the Richards realized their dream of building an orchid garden to showcase specialty plants from around the world. The orchids are enclosed in a half-acre conservatory that is designed as an ever-rotating display. The underlying structure is a tasteful arrangement of bromeliads, palms, and other tropical plants set against a small waterfall and pool. The orchids are overlaid upon this as color schemes, decorative motifs, and botanical displays. Wildlife completes the scene with the pond brimming with koi and tentative chameleons occasionally climbing out on the rocks. Outside the conservatory, the Richards have built a boardwalk through a marshy landscape filled with exotic birds, rare squirrels, and plenty of reeds. A new aviary has recently been added containing color parrots.

GARDEN OPEN: 9:30 am to 4:30 pm Tuesday–Sunday, year-round. ADMISSION: $4.50.

FURTHER INFORMATION FROM: 2501 Old Lake Wilson Road, Kissimmee 34747
(407) 396-1887
www.a-world-of-orchids.com

NEARBY SIGHTS OF INTEREST: Disney World, Citrus Tower

A conservatory showcases orchids from around the globe.

FLORIDA

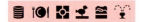

4 Winter Haven: Cypress Gardens

LOCATION: STATE ROUTE 520, OFF U. S. ROUTE 27 AND INTERSTATE 4, BETWEEN DISNEY WORLD AND BUSCH GARDENS

GARDEN OPEN: 9:30 am to 5:00 pm, mid-April–mid-November; 9:30 to 9:00 pm daily, December and January; 9:30 am to 8:00 pm February–mid-April. ADMISSION: $31.95 adults, $27.15 seniors, $14.95 children.

FURTHER INFORMATION FROM: P.O. Box 1, Cypress Gardens 33884
(800) 282-2123
www.cypressgardens.com

NEARBY SIGHTS OF INTEREST: Bok Towers, Fantasy of Flight

Before there was Disney World, Busch Gardens, Sea World, or any of the theme parks that have become synonymous with central Florida, there was Dick Pope's Cypress Gardens. Pope was an energetic entrepreneur and tireless publicist who made a small fortune with the Johnson Outboard engine company. In the 1930s he was inspired by reports of a South Carolina man who had opened his gardens up to the public and made a mint. Pope followed suit, putting together a WPA crew and setting out into the swamps south of Orlando. People thought he was crazy and local support for the project waned, along with WPA dollars. But Pope put himself into Cypress Gardens, literally mucking through the mud, until three years later a floral paradise emerged. The gardens are complete overkill, with bougainvillea, honeysuckle, gardenias, and thousands of exotic tropicals woven together into a lush tapestry. Canals string together the gardens, providing continuity in a continually revolving display. The actual gardens occupy only a fraction of the entire property. Pope understood that to truly make money more was needed than pretty plants, and from the beginning he staged elaborate entertainment events within the gardens to attract attention, such as daredevil ski tricks on Lake Eloise and pretty southern girls dressed up in traditional hoop dresses walking through the grounds. This showmanship has evolved over the years through successive owners, including the publishing conglomerate Harcourt Brace Jovanovich (formerly) and the Busch Entertainment Corporation. Today, Cypress Gardens is in private hands again, and the theme park tradition is vibrant as ever, with a paddle-wheel boat, ice skating, an elevated viewing pavilion, and an aviary all complementing the daredevil skiing. The gardens have grown as well under successive horticulturists. The *Plantation Gardens,* located near the lake, feature herbs and vegetables of southern plantations. The far reaches of the gardens have been developed into a series of theme gardens, including a garden of biblical plants, an *Oriental garden*, a French-inspired formal garden, and a

Mediterranean garden, each presented as a kind of exhibit, almost zoolike in appearance. In the spring the garden hosts a floral show of animal figures crafted in brightly colored flowers—most are quite large, up to 20 feet tall, and adorned with thousands of flowers. The Christmas season witnesses equally unusual feats performed with poinsettias. Perhaps the most stunning feature of the gardens, besides the exotic wildlife, is the stand of ancient cypresses that covers the site and provides a kind of mystique to the otherwise wild fare.

OPPOSITE: *A cornucopia of color cascades down the Mediterranean wall.*

5 Lake Wales: Bok Tower Gardens and Pinewood

LOCATION: BURNS AVENUE, JUST OFF STATE ROUTE 60, THIRTY-FIVE MILES SOUTH OF DISNEY WORLD

There are few stories as thoroughly American as Edward Bok's. Born in the Netherlands, Bok came to New York in 1870 during one of the great waves of European immigration. Educated in Brooklyn public schools, Bok went into publishing with Henry Holt, then Charles Scribner, and finally himself as editor-in-chief of *The Ladies Home Journal*, which he piloted through a meteoric rise. In the 1920s Bok retired to Florida where he managed various philanthropic endeavors, including scholarship programs and citizenship prizes. But the biggest project was the development of a public garden where residents of central Florida could enjoy the natural beauty of their surroundings. Bok hired the Olmsted firm of Boston to lay out a pastoral, parklike landscape garden on the highest rise in Florida, a small knoll called Iron Mountain. On the pinnacle of the hump Bok placed a 205-foot tower, designed by Milton B. Medary of Philadelphia. The tower—constructed in pink and gray Georgian marble and which can be seen from miles away as if drifting in a sea of citrus groves—houses a large carillon, or bell organ. The garden, which was overseen by William Lyman Phillips uses the native Florida plant vocabulary of live oaks, pines, and palms in an English gardenesque manner, with rounded greens of turf, framed vistas, and carefully arced pathways that lead the eye as much as the feet through the landscape. Various reflecting pools and ponds are located at strategic locales, including a quiet, bucolic moat encircling the tower. Several garden rooms and vistas are arranged like quiltwork throughout the landscape. Favorites include the white garden, where newlyweds always get photographed, and the sunset exedra, where expansive views of the surrounding countryside can be imbibed. In all there are 157 acres of tended landscape, which gives over to a nature preserve along one edge.

GARDEN OPEN: 8 am to 5 pm daily, year-round. ADMISSION: $4 adults, $1 children.

FURTHER INFORMATION FROM: 1151 Tower Boulevard, Lake Wales 33853
(941) 676-1408

NEARBY SIGHTS OF INTEREST: Cypress Gardens

Wildlife is abundant and gregarious, such as the squirrels that reportedly crawl into one's pockets uninvited. Adjacent to Bok Towers is Pinewood, the small estate of steel magnate Charles Austin Buck. Buck borrowed Phillips from Bok in 1931 and enlisted his services to create a formal, Mediterranean-themed garden. The bones are deeply Italian, with strong central and crossing axial alleès of citrus trees. The terrace behind the house exudes an ancient feel and overlooks a wilderness in the mode of great Old World estates. A small walled Victorian garden has elements such as a chinoiserie Moon Gate; there are later impressionistic styles, such as the Gertrude Jekyll-inspired blue, white, and yellow garden. If these two gardens seem in contradiction or strong contrast, keep in mind that Phillips soon went on to develop Coral Gables and the art deco Venetian Causeway, linking Miami with the Venetian Islands—two projects that grapple with the spatial and social concerns of picturesque park making within the aesthetic milieu of the Mediterranean revival style so prevalent throughout south Florida.

A judicious use of formal elements anchors the naturalistic atmosphere at Bok Tower.

6 Sarasota: Marie Selby Botanical Gardens

LOCATION: SOUTH PALM AVENUE, AT THE CORNER OF ROUTE U.S. 41, ON THE BAYFRONT

William Selby was heir to the Selby oil fortune (later to evolve into Texaco). He was also a lover of life, and in the first decade of the twentieth century crossed America in a touring car with his equally adventurous wife, Marie. The Selbys made their home on the peninsula in Sarasota, which Marie transformed into a living museum of palms, orchids, and other tropical plants. The most stunning remnant of the Selbys' reign is the *Live Oak Grove* immediately facing the house. Today the immense architecture of the trees supports an exotic collection of epiphytes or "air plants" such as Spanish moss. In fact, when the garden was opened to the public in the 1970s, at Marie's death, the board of directors made a conscious decision to specialize in epiphytes—being the only botanical garden in the country to do so. As a result an entire research facility has grown up around the gardens, as a result, and botanists regularly visit to take advantage of both the grounds and the library. The grounds are still wonderfully maintained as a residential-scaled landscape cultivated with Mrs. Selby's exquisite taste. Behind the house groves of palms and banyans give over the mangroves near the bay. Stitched into the woods are collections of flowering plants, including a display of hibiscus, succulents, and local wildflowers such as helianthus. The displays are arranged around an elliptical walking path. The display house now houses most of the epiphytes, and there is a curatorial staff on-site to provide explanation of these botanical curiosities.

garden open: 10 am to 5 pm daily, except Christmas.
ADMISSION: $8 adults, $4 children 6–11 years.

FURTHER INFORMATION FROM:
811 South Palm Avenue,
Sarasota 34236
(941) 366-5731
www.selby.org

NEARBY SIGHTS OF INTEREST:
Mote Marine Science Center, Ringling Museum

ABOVE: *The tropical house is used for extensive research.*

7 Fort Myers: Edison Estate

LOCATION: MCGREGOR BOULEVARD, BETWEEN ROUTE U. S. 41 AND THE CALOOSAHATCHEE RIVER, DOWNTOWN

GARDEN OPEN: 9 am to 4 pm Monday–Saturday, noon to 4 pm Sunday, year-round except Christmas and Thanksgiving. ADMISSION: free.

FURTHER INFORMATION FROM:
2350 McGregor Boulevard,
Fort Myers 33901
(941) 334-3614
www.edison-ford-estate.com

NEARBY SIGHTS OF INTEREST:
Sanibel Island, Caluso Nature Center

The inventor Thomas Alva Edison first purchased land along the Caloosahatchee River in 1885, during a visit to the west Florida coast with his friend and business partner Ezra Gilliland. The two built matching estates and settled into an easy, summer home relationship with the area. After a falling out with Gilliland, Edison purchased the second home, but in 1916 was joined in the area by his friend Henry Ford, who built a third residence across the street. Edison viewed the compound as his own botanical laboratory and, influenced by the naturalist John Burroughs and the California botanist Luther Burbank (whose empirical methods closely resembled Edison's own), the inventor set about gathering an abundance of exotic tropical plants to assemble on his property. On the eve of World War I Edison became interested in developing a means of harvesting rubber. He tested various plants and eventually discovered a hybridized form of goldenrod that would grow 12 to 18 feet tall. Today the houses are maintained as a museum. The gardens are much the way Edison left them in 1931. An incredible diversity of plant material surrounds the home, including species from Indonesia, South Africa, the Pacific, and the tropical Americas. Owing to Edison's scientific mind, many of the plants have distinct industrial uses and therefore the caretakers warn visitors against touching many of them, as they may be toxic. Edison's wife was responsible for prettifying the garden with several water features as well as a collection of orchids, roses, and bromeliads.

The Edison Estate's enormous banyan tree was planted in 1925, a gift of tire magnate Harvey Firestone.

8 Fort Pierce: Heathcote Botanical Gardens

LOCATION: JUST OFF U. S. ROUTE 1, AT SAVANNAH ROAD

GARDEN OPEN: 9 am to 5 pm Tuesday–Saturday, year-round; 1 pm to 5 pm Sunday, November– April. **ADMISSION:** $3 adults, $1 children.

FURTHER INFORMATION FROM: 210 Savannah Road, Fort Pierce 34982 (561) 464-4672

NEARBY SIGHTS OF INTEREST: Fort Lucie Museum, Lake Okeechobee

Heathcote was begun in the 1950s when Jim and Mollie Crummins relocated their nursery business from the other side of town. They brought with them their 1922 cottage and set about transforming the property to their liking, including developing an intimate Japanese garden adjacent to the house. In the 1980s when the property, which had fallen into disuse, was threatened by a road development, a group of concerned citizens banded together to save what was left of the Japanese garden. As a result of their labor a formalized botanical garden has been created at Heathcote. The *Japanese Garden* has been fully restored and features a quiet strolling path that ambles through a lush tropical planting. A narrow, craggy *Lily Pond*, choked with foliage, lies at the center, while such small architectural features as stone lanterns and elegant bridges provide focal points. A permanent display of bonsais is also located here. The gardens, understandably, have taken a while to get on their feet. At present the main attractions are the well-maintained palm forest, a woodland of native plants, and several border gardens of bromeliads. Two recent additions include a children's garden, featuring playful topiaries fitted into the landscape to create surprise, and a memorial garden. This is a quiet, snug space oriented around a circular plaza. The cool shade and mellow tones of green are intended to create a spiritual ambience where garden visitors might remember a loved one. Heathcote is a humble but beautiful place, particularly in the height of summer when a vibrant border of ginger comes to life. At other times the Japanese garden provides an unwavering presence in this rapidly growing suburban region.

ABOVE: *The Heathcote Gardens are an oasis in Florida's burgeoning suburban landscape.*

FLORIDA

GARDEN OPEN: 8:30 am to 4:30 pm Monday–Saturday, 1 pm to 5 pm Sunday, year-round. ADMISSION: free.

FURTHER INFORMATION FROM:
531 North Military Trail, West Palm Beach 33415
(561) 233-1749

NEARBY SIGHTS OF INTEREST:
Flagler Museum

A handsome boardwalk serves to immerse us in the native flora at Mounts.

9 West Palm Beach: Mounts Botanical Garden

LOCATION: MILITARY TRAIL AT ELIZABETH STREET, JUST NORTH OF SOUTHERN BOULEVARD (U. S. ROUTE 98) AND NEAR THE AIRPORT

In 1914 Congress passed a law that every land-grant college must create an extension service the purpose of which was to bring some of the information and knowledge generated in the schools to the communities. Marvin "Red" Mounts was an agent of the University of Florida's extension in Palm Beach for over fifty years. Red's great contribution was horticultural, and in addition to the educational services that the university provided, he developed a small garden where residents could learn about plants and botanical science. Since Mount's retirement in 1965 the garden has continued to grow and be formalized into a true public garden. With over 13 acres, it is a fairly large place with a good-sized collection of tropical plants. Fruit trees dominate the garden. Besides avocados, bananas, and mangos, the garden contains many strange and exotic specimens, including Jaboticaba, Grumichama, Atemoya, and Ylang ylang, a southeast Asian tree used in the recipe for Chanel No. 5. The front area of the garden is arranged as a series of educational exhibits. Special attractions include a display of poisonous plants and a rainforest landscape overflowing with bananas. Immediately adjacent to the visitor center is a small rose garden. Deeper into the garden larger landscape themes emerge. A walking path through indigenous Florida forest encloses a small lake. Along the way we pass beneath a bucolic bougainvillea arbor and constantly catch glimpses of an island that serves as a canvas for all species of groundcover. The garden also reflects a growing awareness of ecology in gardening, and in addition to the general displays of native plants there is a Xeriscape garden that showcases techniques for minimizing water consumption and the use of harmful herbicides in a typical residential garden.

10 Fort Lauderdale: Flamingo Gardens

LOCATION: FLAMINGO ROAD, OFF I-595 (EAST OF I-95), NEAR THE INTERSECTION WITH GRIFFIN ROAD

Floyd and Jane Wray settled on this tract of slight upland on the edge of the Everglades swamp in 1926 at the height of the great migration into the Miami area. Within a decade the 2,000-acre property was under cultivation as a citrus farm for export of fresh, mass-produced oranges to northern states. The Wrays were keenly interested in the native flora and fauna of their adopted home (they had arrived from Michigan) and set aside 12 acres for a botanical garden planted with a wide variety of botanicals in a naturalistic manner. The proximity of the Everglades and the garden's diversity combined to attract a lot of exotic birds. Today, after a well-tended preservation, Flamingo Gardens is also known as an exceptional aviary. Palms form the backbone of the gardens, although there are also incredible samples of bromeliads and ferns. Along the walking paths, the ground plane is planted with ginger, fruits, and birds of paradise. The bird sanctuary, a 60-acre landscape of mangrove swamp, cypress forest, and tropical hardwood hammock, takes in actual birds that have somehow become sick or injured. Flamingoes, of course, abound; good observers will also spot the endangered wood stork. Although one doesn't typically associate the abundantly wet lowlands of southern Florida with water shortages, intensive farming and wasteful development trends have threatened the groundwater supply. In response the Flamingo Gardens also includes a Xeriscape garden, which showcases ways to maintain a tropical garden through the careful selection of plants and without over-irrigating. There are still plenty of citrus trees on the property, and visitors are encouraged to sample the local crop on a shaded patio before heading home.

HOUSE OPEN: 9:30 am to 4:30 pm daily. Garden open: 9:30 am to 5:30 pm daily. ADMISSION: $10 adults, $5 children 6–12 years, free children five years and under.

FURTHER INFORMATION FROM:
3251 South Miami Avenue, Miami 33129
(305) 250-9133

NEARBY SIGHTS OF INTEREST:
Lowe Art Museum, Miami Museum of Science

Bird of paradise

FLORIDA

11 Miami: Vizcaya

LOCATION: SOUTH MIAMI DRIVE, EXIT 1 ON I-95, FOUR MILES SOUTH OF DOWNTOWN MIAMI

The Basque word *vizcaya* means "elevated place," and has several connotations at this estate on Biscayne Bay. Not only does it connect the property to that northern Spanish province on the shores of the Bay of Biscay, but the word also seems to refer at once to the natural topography, architectural grandeur, and spiritual presence of the house and its magnificent gardens. Industrialist John Deering began construction of Vizcaya in 1914 when Miami was a small city of 10,000 people. For several years he traveled through Europe with painter and interior designer Paul Chalfin who became his artistic consultant and general contractor. Together they purchased art and architectural ornaments from crumbling castles and manors throughout France and Italy. Unlike so many other estates created in this manner that seem haphazardly to display the plunder of classical Europe for the sake of displaying plunder, the disparate styles and aesthetics at Vizcaya are knitted together by a single, coherent vision: to recreate an Italianate villa as if it had been built in the swamps of Florida almost 400 years ago.

Surrounding the opulent house are ten acres of gardens designed by Colombian-born landscape architect Diego Suarez. Having thoroughly engrossed himself in baroque gardens during his studies in Florence, Suarez created an intricate, stylized, and highly controlled landscape that epitomizes the height of neoclassical tastes in the early decades of the twentieth century. The gardens proceed from the south facade of the house, looking out to excellent vistas of the landscape. Arranged along a central axis are a series of major design features intended to draw the eye to successive layers of the landscape. In the foreground lies a central reflecting pool enclosing a slight mound of greenery set like a kind of topographical island. Beyond this a stone staircase encased in flowing water rises the *Mount,* an artificial hummock adorned at its peak with an ornate Italianate gazebo. The succession is carefully choreographed. The ground plane is a sharp terrace of green supporting a series of linear interventions—an alleè of topiaries, the staircase, and then balustrades upon the Mount. Each piece seems fashioned for its place, not gathered from somewhere else, and as the eye travels through the space, the layers appear seamless.

At one time the landscape kept unfolding on the other side of the hill, but over the years parts of the estate were sold off. The contemporary gardens continue to

HOUSE OPEN: 9:30 am to 4:30 pm daily. Garden open: 9:30 am to 5:30 pm daily. **ADMISSION:** $10 adults, $5 children 6–12 years, free children five years and under.

FURTHER INFORMATION FROM:
3251 South Miami Avenue, Miami 33129
(305) 250-9133

NEARBY SIGHTS OF INTEREST:
Lowe Art Museum, Miami Museum of Science

OPPOSITE: *Floating on the edge of Biscayne Bay is the ornate palace Vizcaya.*

BELOW: *Ornaments from European estates created the architecture of the gardens.*

Statuary and baroque details set the ambiance.

BELOW: *The Italian influenced Fountain Garden*

the east of The Mount, each confined to a small island in the bay just a throw from the shore. The *Maze Garden* performs a riff on an old idea, substituting native orange jasmine in place of boxwood typical of the Italian tradition. Descending from the Mount, a golden path leads into the *Fountain Garden*, a terrace focused in upon a travertine fountain that dates to the seventeenth century. At the far end lies a Roman altar from the second century. Throughout the gardens are various European statues.

Framing the east "lawn" of water just before the house is the rococo *Great Stone Barge,* a confused admixture of architecture and sculpture that rests in a small bay just off a terrace of the house. The barge serves the practical purpose of breaking wave action. But its presence is overwhelmingly visual. Carved obelisks, swirling balustrades, and a rustic stone base reflect the early morning sun and calm the waters that lap against the bay edge. The terrace that faces the Barge is a stretched horizontal space, perfectly balanced by statuary. Tucked into one corner is the *Secret Garden,* a kind of hidden grotto situated in the middle of the hubbub. Novelties were a significant feature in Italian gardens, and at Vizcaya this is embodied by the *Theater Garden,* a small olive-shaped architectural space set on a small pierhead. Its purpose is fanciful and aesthetic rather than for performances. The last island space set along the bay's edge is the ornate tea house, capped with a latticed dome and one of the cooler places at the end of a summer's day.

When the gardens were first designed they exhibited a kind of hyperkinesis, moving from one planting scheme to another. The place is still outstanding, but the last few plantings have been altered slightly and floral arrangements toned down. The house, conversely, has retained its originally eclectic spirit. Chalfin laid the two floors out almost museumlike, with each room leading into the next. A central courtyard ties the spaces together spatially. It is an arcaded space, marked in the center by a large marble dolphin and planted with delicate groundcover.

FLORIDA

12 Miami: Fairchild Tropical Garden

LOCATION: LE JEUNE ROAD (SW 42ND AVENUE) SOUTH OF MIAMI TO OLD CUTLER ROAD, NINE MILES SOUTH OF THE AIRPORT

In the 1920s Miami exploded. By 1926 the boom—with a capital *B*, as a local historian calls it—was adding up to 6,000 new residents each day. One of these, David Fairchild, a botanist and plant explorer, had spent his career searching the globe for new exotic plants. Fairchild introduced into the United States mangos, alfalfa, horseradish, and flowering cherry trees. When Fairchild retired to Miami in 1935 he made the acquaintance of Colonel Robert Montgomery, a successful south Florida businessman who had a passion for exotic plants. He also had a vision of a large public garden to adorn this new city, and together the two men set out to make it happen. The original design of the Fairchild garden was completed by William Lyman Phillips, a Miami landscape architect who had worked during his early years in the office of Frederick Law Olmsted, designer of Central Park in New York City. In Florida, Phillips was responsible for the design of numerous parks and small towns, and the curving cul-de-sacs and thoroughfares, coupled with formal alleès of palms are reminiscent of the grand island parkways and entrances of places like Coral Gables and Key Biscayne.

Fairchild's impact on the garden was immediate and lasting. Backed by the colonel's financial support, in 1940 he embarked on a sailing expedition to Indonesia that yielded a great deal of material, including an array of palms, cycads, and tropical specimens. By 1950 the garden was expansive, featuring a mature arboretum of palms, called the *Montgomery Palmetum*, an amphitheater, a library and museum, and an extensive network of trails and paths winding around a system of fourteen lakes. All this provided the naturalistic backdrop for several garden areas, including the sunken garden—a limestone hollow planted with ferns and aroids and featuring a small waterfall—and the *Vine Pergola*, a 560-foot-long arbor covered with various flowering plants. One of the most striking features is the *Bailey Palm Glade*, a stonescaped garden of indigenous and exotic palms arranged around rugged stone steps and walls. Since the time of Montgomery, Phillips, and Fairchild the garden has evolved into one of most important south Florida gardens, with extensive collections of bamboo, a conservatory of orchids, bromeliads, and ferns, and a rainforest habitat. Ecosystem gardens have become a preoccupation over the last ten

GARDEN OPEN: 9:30 am to 4:30 pm daily, year-round, except Christmas day.
ADMISSION: $8 adults, free children under 12 years.

FURTHER INFORMATION FROM:
10901 Old Cutler Road,
Miami 33156
(305) 667-1651
www.ftg.org

NEARBY SIGHTS OF INTEREST:
Parrot Jungle, Vizcaya

An international collection of palms forms the backbone of Fairchild Tropical Garden.

years, and today the garden features one of the best collections of rare and endangered plants of south Florida as well as an exhibit of Bahamian ones. Unusual for botanical gardens, there are also several cultural displays, including an authentic dwelling of the Chachi people who live in the Ecuadorian rainforest and a garden of Mayan fruits and vegetables.

GARDEN OPEN: 10 am to 5 pm daily, year-round. **ADMISSION:** $6.

FURTHER INFORMATION FROM:
One Free School Lane, Key West 33040
(305) 294-0015
www.Hurricanecenter.com/secretgarden

NEARBY SIGHTS OF INTEREST:
Hemingway House, Key West Aquarium

13 Key West: Nancy Forrester's Secret Garden

LOCATION: FREE SCHOOL LANE, OFF SIMONTON STREET, BETWEEN FLEMING AVENUE AND SOUTHARD AVENUE, DOWNTOWN

As old bohemian Key West vanishes under a hail of strip malls and new suburban developments, there remain several pockets of its iconoclasm hidden beneath this new-fangled exterior. One of these is Nancy Forrester's Secret Garden, which has been profiled by Charles Kurralt and garden writer Alan Lacy as one of the best forgotten spots in the area. Yet tourists seem more inclined to frequent the new coffee shops of the rapidly gentrifying town than to venture into these wilds; and rest assured that on most days you will have the gardens to yourself. Forrester began this garden thirty years ago, and after a lengthy gestation period opened it up to the public in 1994. The garden is effusively planted with palms, which create a cavernous, jungle effect. Many in the venerable collection (150 specimens in all) are from exotic equatorial regions, such as the Marquesa Islands and Madagascar, and cannot survive even in Miami. The garden is designed as a tightly packed jungle space, cut through with a curving path. Several tables and chairs provide places to sit and enjoy the scene, which Forrester and a team of volunteer artists have carefully evolved over the years. Some visitors have protested the lack of labeling, and considering the amount unusual and exotic plant material this is probably a failure of sorts. But Forrester is interested in something else entirely. She speaks about over-development, encroaching concrete, and her own sense of detachment from the land that increases with every new condominium in town. Key West, for its part, has been fighting to demolish the garden and build time-share condominiums. But until that day, the garden is meant to be a spiritual, relaxing place where one can relish an otherworldly collection of flora. Besides the palms, many of which are enormous, the garden features a wealth of orchids, colorful bromeliads, yellow and fire-red heliconias, and all sorts of other mysteries that even Forrester struggles to remember by their correct botanical distinction. What she does recall are the wild attributes: there are the fluorescent orange mushrooms that

Close-up of Nancy Forrestor's exotic collection.

often appear after a rain, and the plant that blooms for a single day and suffocates the garden in a stench that she describes as "like a big dead cow." While her tastes, after all these years, are piqued by the bizarre, the garden appeals to all types—even those unaccustomed to the tropics. Forrester is shy and eschews marketing the garden. But as the only true garden in Key West, it would be a crime to forgo a visit during a vacation there.

14 Key West: Audubon House and Tropical Gardens

LOCATION: WHITEHEAD STREET, AT GREENE, IN THE OLD TOWN

GARDEN OPEN: 9:30 am to 5:00 pm daily. ADMISSION: $8.50 adults, $7.50 seniors, $5.00 students, $3.50 children.

FURTHER INFORMATION FROM: 205 Whitehead Street, Key West 33040
(305) 294-2116
www.audubonhouse.com

NEARBY SIGHTS OF INTEREST: Hemingway House

Few historic houses are named for a visitor rather than an owner. When the visitor was John James Audubon and the property has been given over to botanica such as the great naturalist might have found during one of his many stays, then it seems to make sense. The Audubon House was actually built by sea captain John Huling Geiger and his wife Lucretia in 1820. In the 1950s its owners decided to use the property as an interpretive exhibit where the diverse floral history of the island could be displayed. Up until 1941, when a pipeline was constructed from the mainland, water was a serious commodity, necessitating that every residence on the island be built with a rainwater catchment basin. Here it is located beneath the large terrace constructed at the rear of the house. The plantings that enclose the terrace and then extend into the far reaches of the small lot suggest antiquity, a time when settlers first came to the island and brought with them vegetables and other plants fitted for survival, but also more recent history when plant explorers and naturalists brought to the island exotic tropicals from elsewhere. Thus we find an eclectic mix of the pragmatic and esoteric. Of the former there are many outstanding specimens in the garden, including arrowroot (used by natives to make starch), monstera (that produces a corncob-shaped edible fruit), and loquat (a fruit used as a sedative). The Victorian, fanciful influences on Key West are apparent in the orchids, tree-bound bromeliads, and African and Asian tropicals, such as pentas, pygmy date palms, and the dynamic snake plant that folds its leaves during the heat of the day. The nursery is a historic structure in which the garden's horticulturists have been experimenting with medicinal plants from Central America and the West Indies. The gardens are laid out around a pleasant circuit of old brick paths punctuated by iron seats every once in a while. The house is set up as a period museum with furnishings marking the entire twentieth century and drawn from auctions and estates around the world, as well as 28 engravings by Audubon.

TOP: *Exotic tropicals on the island*

BOTTOM: *Audobon House, built by sea captain John Huling Geiger in 1820*

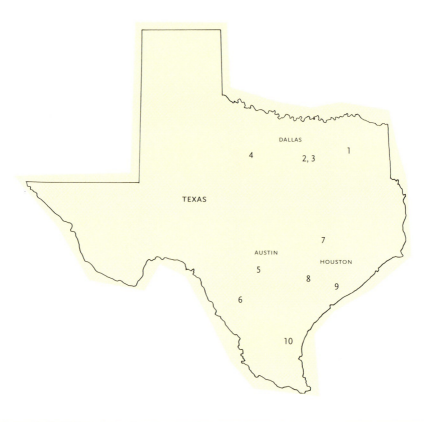

1 Tyler: Tyler Rose Gardens
2 Dallas: Dallas Arboretum
3 Dallas: Dallas Horticulture Center
4 Fort Worth: Fort Worth Botanic Gardens
5 Austin: Lady Bird Johnson Wildflower Center
6 San Antonio: San Antonio Botanical Garden
7 Humble: Mercer Arboretum
8 Houston: Bayou Bend Gardens
9 Galveston: Moody Gardens
10 Corpus Christi: Corpus Christi Botanical Garden

TEXAS

It has always been disputed whether Texas is part of the South. Many feel the issue was decided by the Civil War when the state joined the Confederacy. It is probably more properly considered apart—and even then the eastern and western halves of the state are so completely different that it even makes sense to think of them separately.

The hills east of Dallas are wonderfully rich in history and culture. The one garden in this region, the Tyler Rose Garden, is a symbolic garden. It embodies this small town's gracious history as the capital of roses. It also provides residents with a municipal park of incomparable beauty in the heart of town. Moving east we find ourselves in the urban sprawl of Dallas and Fort Worth. Three public gardens compete here for preeminence. For many the Dallas Arboretum and Botanical Gardens wins the fight. Nestled onto the side of White Rock Lake, the gardens are the fruition of many years' desire among Dallas residents to create a major public garden. The WPA-era Horticulture Center, on the other hand, has been an institution for many years. Each garden presents a different picture of gardening. The arboretum is a contemporary garden, designed with a sensitivity for landscape nuance. The center, in contrast, began as a typical post-Victorian American garden—the prototypical public rose garden. But lately it has adopted a more ecological stance.

These two themes, art and science, are too rarely melded. But in the incomparable Lady Bird Johnson Wildflower Center poetry and ecology join. This garden, led by the indefatigable former first lady who for the last thirty years has spearheaded beautification initiatives across the country, is at the forefront of the native plants revolution. Almost every wilderness garden in the country has some tie with this organization, as it administers a large database of research material.

OPPOSITE: *Lady Bird Johnson Wildflower Center*

The one traditional estate garden is Bayou Bend, the former home of Ima Hogg. It is a Texas estate of the highest order and testifies to Houston's stature as the most cosmopolitan area in the state. Paradoxically one of Hogg's great acquaintances was Henry F. du Pont, the consummate naturalistic gardener who created Winterthur in Delaware. Bayou Bend is a stark contrast to Winterthur, and presents the classical traditions of garden design.

The last garden in the book is perhaps the most optimistic. The Corpus Christi Botanical Garden is a small garden—maybe seeming inconsequential. But great things are occurring there. Not only is the little place expanding, but it is bringing attention back to the surrounding landscape, showing people the existence of nature in their backyard. This is probably the ultimate purpose of gardens in our time.

Tyler: Tyler Rose Garden

LOCATION: GLENWOOD STREET AND FRONT STREET, NEAR STATE ROUTE 155, DOWNTOWN

GARDEN OPEN: dawn to dusk daily. ADMISSION: free.

FURTHER INFORMATION FROM: 420 Rose Park Drive, Tyler 75702
(903) 531-1200

NEARBY SIGHTS OF INTEREST: Bonner-Whitaker-McClendon House

For many years Tyler, Texas, was America's rose capital, its local farms producing almost a fifth of the roses in the country and yet possessing not a single public rose garden. Admonished by visiting rosarians for this oversight, the city finally built itself a large municipal rose park in the 1950s. The old part of the garden is vaguely formal, with a large central fountain and the roses set out in radiating beds. The original stock was supplied by local nurseries with varieties shipped in from Philadelphia and other major rose centers. Each year the collection is augmented with new plants to keep it fresh and inviting. In 1995 the garden became a testing site for new roses, and an entirely new area was developed. Although it has a kind of antiseptic layout—more suitable for the scientific method of developing new varieties—the array of visual and olfactory presentations is overwhelming. There are thousands of different roses covering the entire garden during the summer in a sea of undulating color. Many are named after celebrities, such as Dolly Parton, sometimes because of certain attributes, and others because of a social connection. Perhaps the most fascinating part of the garden is the *Rose Center*, which features an exhibit on the history of the rose, including all sorts of arcana relating to rose festivals, rose queens, and the ways roses have come to form an important anchor in civic life. Suddenly the rose seems so much more than a simple flower.

Acres of olfactory manna— the Tyler Rose Garden.

TEXAS

GARDEN OPEN: 10 am to 6 pm daily, March–October, 10 am to 5 pm, November–February.
ADMISSION: free.

FURTHER INFORMATION FROM:
8525 Garland Road, Dallas 75218
(214) 327-8263

NEARBY SIGHTS OF INTEREST:
Bath House Cultural Center, Biblical Arts Center

2 Dallas: Dallas Arboretum and Botanical Garden

LOCATION: WHITE ROCK LAKE, AT GARLAND ROAD AND BUCKNER BOULEVARD, SEVEN MILES EAST OF DOWNTOWN

Dallas Arboretum and Botanical Garden is located on the site of the former estate of Everette Lee DeGolyer, a prominent Dallas citizen who lobbied hard for a public garden throughout the twentieth century. The underlying structure of the gardens, which occupy thirty-three acres, is parkland developed by DeGolyer. Overlaid on this are sumptuous formal gardens. The heart of the display is the *Jonsson Color Garden*, a fabulous assemblage of bulbs and flowering azaleas, including 20,000 azaleas. The beds are laid out in a meandering fashion beneath a light canopy of oaks that line White Rock Lake. This has a calming effect on what might otherwise be a somewhat overwrought display. Instead, it is magical, with a symphony of perennials evolving through the season. In contrast, there is also a native plants display in the *Lay Ornamental Garden*. Since Dallas borders the eastern and western United States, the associations seem to nod each way, with plenty of herbaceous varieties common to the deciduous forest east of here and the beginning of the scrub of the west. Over the years an energetic volunteer force, wealthy donors, and several important designers have aligned to develop a series of wonderful formal gardens, including an English cottage style garden, an allée of magnolias, a rose garden, and a grotto garden that features a collection of figurative bronzes engulfed by leafy ferns. The newest addition is *A Woman's Garden*, designed by Boston landscape architect Morgan Wheelock. According to the designer the garden administration wanted a formal, controlled space, but upon investigation Morgan found that natural conditions were very sensual. On top of this, the space needed to exude feminine qualities. The resulting design is a yin-yang approach, with a little of everything wrapped together. The pathway winds through a series of rooms that are largely meditative. Sculptural pieces, including a wind harp, complement the scene. One of the more interesting spaces is an area that demonstrations the life cycle of trees, called the *nurturing garden*.

The meditative pathway through A Woman's Garden

3 Dallas: Dallas Horticulture Center

LOCATION: TWO MILES FROM DOWNTOWN

Perhaps the least static thing in this world—aside from nature itself—is a garden. Actually, a garden—since it arises from the hands of humans—may be more dynamic. In any case, the Dallas Horticulture Center is a wonderful place to see this dynamism in action. Over the last forty years, since its inception during World War II the garden has evolved from a traditional showcase for "modern" horticultural trends—including displays of exotics and European-inspired garden design—to a repository for one of the best native plant collections. At the center of the garden are the historic gardens: an antique rose collection bounded by perennial borders, a *physic garden* containing medicinal and industrial plants, a *Shakespeare Garden* with botanical selections drawn from the bard's writings, and an enormous, world-class iris garden. The *Texas Native Plants Collection* complements these with an offering of wildflowers and woody plants. Dallas occupies an unusual place on what is called Edwards Plateau, a kind of border land where the verdant, rolling topography of the east melds into the more arid landscape of the west—and the plant palette reflects this intermediate zone. In addition to an onsite conservatory, the architectural core of the garden is an allée lined by hollies and leading to a geyser.

GARDEN OPEN: dawn to dusk daily, year-round. ADMISSION: free.

FURTHER INFORMATION FROM:
3601 Martin Luther King Boulevard, Dallas 75315
(214) 428-7476

NEARBY SIGHTS OF INTEREST:
Dallas Museum of Art

The grande allée culminates in a classic expression.

TEXAS

GARDEN OPEN: 8 am to dusk daily, year-round. ADMISSION: fee varies for different gardens.

FURTHER INFORMATION FROM: 3220 Botanic Garden Boulevard, Fort Worth 76107 (817) 871-7689

NEARBY SIGHTS OF INTEREST: Will Rogers Memorial Center

4 Fort Worth: Fort Worth Botanic Gardens

LOCATION: EXIT 12 ON INTERSTATE 30, DOWNTOWN

In the 1930s the Works Progress Administration used gardens, among other things, as a way to employ people. And although so many of these gardens have disappeared there are still a number of wonderful public gardens in the country that date from this era—such as the Fort Worth Botanic Garden. Reflecting the period, a large rose garden was made the central element of the botanic gardens when they were first designed. The rose garden is classically appointed with a radial design and hundreds, if not thousands, of bushes—a condition owing as much to the general craze in America for this plant as the surplus of labor at the time. The full spectrum of classic *Rosa* is represented including miniatures, creepers, and a handsome (and odoriferous) heirloom garden. Outside of this, many other intimate spaces have blossomed in the garden over its 60-year history. The Japanese garden is a favorite, oriented around a precious lake with a Texan palette of ornamental grasses and native stone cupping the edge. A small bridge and a few architectural pieces let you know you're in an Asian setting, while color and texture evoke a more regional idea. The garden was designed by Kingsley Wu, and features a tea house and viewing pavilion. The conservatory features a bulb garden in its center and educational displays line the perimeter.

The teahouse in fall

5 Austin: Lady Bird Johnson Wildflower Center

LOCATION: HIGHWAY 1 SOUTH, NINE MILLES SOUTH OF THE CITY, AT LA CROSSE STREET

If the native plant revolution can be traced to a single cause—a difficult task considering that the ecology movement and natural changes in garden design aesthetics have both been major influences—one would have to look to the National Wildflower Center in Austin. Founded in the early 1980s by Lady Bird Johnson and a couple of like-minded naturalists, the center has been a forceful proponent of preserving and restoring America's vanishing landscapes. Exhibit one is the center's own garden, which sits at the far eastern end of the Edwards Plateau, a rolling ridge that cuts through the heart of the state. The plateau marks the boundary zone between the midwestern prairie, the Chihuahua desert, and the southern woodlands, at a kind of junction of vibrant landscapes. Unfortunately its naturally verdant topography, once covered with meadows of wildflowers, has been altered by human habitation—particularly by the absence of periodic burning that once kept invasives at bay. Today the large meadow of wildflowers occupying the northeast corner of the garden epitomizes the center's mission, which is to re-establish the presettlement flora that once characterized the region.

GARDEN OPEN: 9:00 am to 5:30 pm Tuesday–Sunday.
ADMISSION: $4.00 adults, $2.50 students and seniors.

FURTHER INFORMATION FROM:
4801 La Crosse Avenue, Austin 78739
(512) 292-4200
www.wildflower.org

NEARBY SIGHTS OF INTEREST:
LBJ Library, Ney Museum

The outlying landscape is a testing ground for native plants.

TOP: *A wildflower display illustrates how these bluebonnets can be used in home gardens.*

BOTTOM: *The iconic tower presides over the display gardens at the Ladybird Wildflower Center*

The garden experience begins in the welcome center where you get a quick but thorough education in native plants—the concept in general and central Texas species in particular. The reception area is oriented around a courtyard garden, designed in a typically Spanish manner, with a stone terrace, planters, and geometric arrangement of plants.

However the actual material has been carefully chosen from a palette of natives. Beyond the courtyard is a pleasantly arched space called the *Seed Garden*. The idea here is to transition away from the formalism of the courtyard and into a more flowing, naturalistic landscape. Although still confined by the buildings and pathway, the approach is derivative of Roberto Burle-Marx's inspired use of contrasting textures and forms. Again the palette is pure Texas natives, with a strong emphasis on grasses.

Home idea gardens might be considered the most uninteresting attribute of public gardens. But at the Wildflower Center the display gardens are designed to make some very specific philosophical points, and because they do this so convincingly they earn high marks. Three separate terraces comprise the space. On one is a traditional suburban Texas yard, with non-native shrubs and trees and plenty of finely groomed, herbicide-hungry turf grass. The next two terraces present ways to do the same thing using native species. The first option is grotesquely suburban, while the second is more "naturalistic"; both make the point that there are viable options to the unsustainable suburban yard.

The grand conclusion of the floral collection is the large rounded meadow adjacent to the center where the staff tests various kinds of wildflowers. By definition this is a continually evolving space—at times filled with bands of bright color, at others graying into a winter meadow, or assuming the golden sheen of landscape in transition. The program dictates a kind of scientific approach, and yet for the visitor the space retains a kind of natural, sublime beauty. Partly this is due to a kind of

Duchamp-esque heightening of awareness. The field might normally be seen as a pretty but not striking meadow of wildflowers, yet here assumes an etherealtiy, because it is cupped by the land and seemingly put upon a pedestal for viewing the wildflower garden.

One of the subtler lessons of the Wildflower Center has to do with water conservation. Runoff is a terribly destructive force, scraping and eroding soil and carrying pollutants into drinking water. Most of the time runoff is directed into a low-lying area, but this is like gargling instead of brushing: your breath may smell all right, but sooner or later your teeth will fall out. The center, in the spirit of proactive environmentalism that pervades the entire place, has turned its gardening eyes to the most unlikely of places, the parking lot, and re-designed it with a water-conscious design. Runoff is reduced by permeable paving and detention basins filled with intermittent wetland species.

This description is not intended to make the garden sound pedantic; it is a beautiful place that speaks as much about the poetry of native landscape as it does about its science. Possibly the most important contribution it makes to the culture at large, in fact, is to unite these things and refuse to deal with them separately.

A close-up of Gaillardia pulchella.

Interesting nooks show how design and native plants integrate.

6 San Antonio: San Antonio Botanical Garden

GARDEN OPEN: 9 am to 6 pm daily, April–October; 8 am to 5 pm daily, November–March.
ADMISSION: $5 adults, $2 seniors, $1 children.

FURTHER INFORMATION FROM:
5555 Funston Place,
San Antonio
(210) 207-3259

NEARBY SIGHTS OF INTEREST:
McNay Art Museum

Pines, yucca, mesquite, and magnolias on a walk through the San Antonio Botanical Garden

LOCATION: OFF BRAUNFELS ROAD, MIDWAY BETWEEN DOWNTOWN AND AIRPORT

San Antonio sits at a geographic crossroads between several landscapes, where the gentle deciduous forest of the East rolls into the plains of the West, and where the hills of the North pancake out into the deserts of the South. The garden takes these varied transitions as its *parti* and uses a wondrously diverse collection of native plants coupled with architectural accents to describe a kind of "walk across Texas." Even the weeds are accentuated, down to the poison ivy of the East, as we roll west from pines and magnolias to yucca and mesquite. The gardens were first planted in 1980 and although young have been well cared for. The conservatory, designed by Emilio Ambasz and built in 1990, offers a striking architectural contrast. Most of the structure is buried beneath ground with only the roofline jutting above. It contains a full range of greenhouse climates, from alpine to desert to tropical. The palm house, capped with a roof that looks like a glass volcano, is masterful with 110 different species. In the center of the structure is a lovely sunken garden planted with aquatics. The formal gardens include a rose garden, a garden for the blind, and a Japanese Garden designed by the master Koishi Yasui and built by a crew of Japanese gardeners. It is so authentic that the San Antonio Botanical Garden had to get permission from Japanese officials before building it.

7 Humble: Mercer Arboretum and Botanic Garden

LOCATION: OFF HARDY TOLL ROAD, TWENTY-FIVE MILES NORTH OF HOUSTON

Thelma Mercer and her husband Charles developed these gardens over a lifetime. They comprise 262 acres, the core of which features wonderfully informal gardens. The Mercers were interested in ecological associations, and used land forms and water to create a maze of different areas. In the *Dryland Garden* water is drained quickly and the plant palette ventures far afield toward west Texas and more arid varieties. The *Tropical Garden* has a small rain forest designed in a zone that is normally considered subtropical. Finally we come to the rich tapestry of naturalized bulbs that compose the *Daylily Garden*.

GARDEN OPEN: 8 am to 7 pm daily, April–October; 8 am to 5 pm daily, November–March. **ADMISSION:** free.

FURTHER INFORMATION FROM:
22306 Aldine-Westfield Road, Humble 77338
(281) 443-8731

NEARBY SIGHTS OF INTEREST:
Lower Houston State Park

Mercer Aroboretum's Daylily Garden

8 Houston: Bayou Bend Gardens

GARDEN OPEN: 10:00 am to 5:00 pm Tuesday–Saturday, 1:00 pm to 5:00 pm Sunday.
ADMISSION: $3 adults.
MUSEUM TOURS: 10:00 am to 2:45 pm Tuesday–Friday, 10:00 am to 11:15 pm Sunday.
ADMISSION: $10.00 adults, $8.50 seniors, $5.00 children.

FURTHER INFORMATION FROM:
1 Westcott Street, Houston 77007
(713) 639-7750

NEARBY SIGHTS OF INTEREST: Cullen Sculpture Garden, The Menil Collection

LOCATION: WESTCOTT STREET, JUST OFF MEMORIAL DRIVE, ON THE NORTHWEST SIDE OF DOWNTOWN

Ima Hogg was the daughter of Jim Hogg, governor of Texas and one of the state's earliest oil prospectors. Although he never saw the wealth bubble from the ground of his Texas estate, his children came of age blessed not only with wealth but culture as well. Miss Hogg (she never married) possessed exquisite taste. And like her good friend Henry du Pont, she acquired an exceptional collection of American decorative arts. She housed the collection in a mansion designed by Texan architect John Staub. The house was named Bayou Bend, as it stood on a high, wooded tract of land in the elbow of lazy Buffalo Bayou. In addition to arts collecting, Hogg shared another deep passion with du Pont: gardening. Unlike du Pont, who reveled in naturalistic horticulture, Hogg's tastes ran more toward European traditions. Arranged around the mansion are eight formal gardens, cut and divided by parterres and planted with all sorts of wonderfully maintained ornamental flower beds. A rich palette of flowering shrubs—crepe myrtle, magnolias, and azaleas, overlays the green structure of each garden. Several are oriented upon a marble statue—Clio (the muse of history), Euterpe (the muse of music), and Diana (the huntress). Native plants fill out one of the gardens which is designed in the shape of the Texas star. Beyond the confines of the formal gardens the property opens up into lovely woodlands. It was du Pont who suggested that Hogg transform her property into a public museum, much as he had done at Winterthur. The house contains an incredible collection of Americana, while the gardens still reign on their little woody knoll above the bayou.

The Diana Garden at the Museum of Fine Arts, Houston Bayou Bend

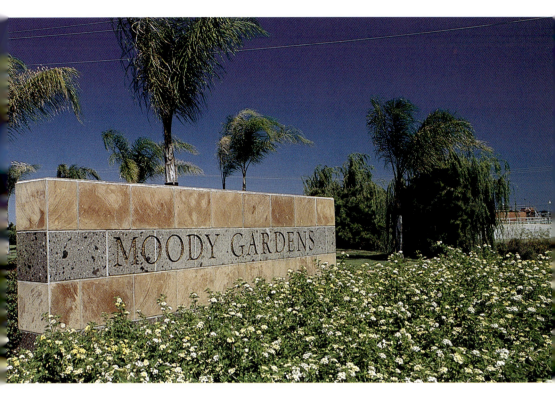

Galveston: Moody Gardens

LOCATION: HOPE BOULEVARD, SOUTH OF HOUSTON

Moody Gardens was established in 1986 by Robert L. Moody who had suffered a head injury in a car accident and discovered rehabilitative horseback riding, called hippotherapy (using the motion and balance of a horse's gait to stimulate human neuro-musclar improvements). Moody started the gardens as a therapeutic endeavor, which quickly evolved to include a strong horticultural component. Today there is a little bit of theme park element, with the introduction of various space-themed areas. But the gardens still remain the main feature. The *Rainforest Pyramid* is a large glasshouse planted with the exotic flora of Asia, Africa, and the Americas. The canopy is a startling 55 feet tall, with lush vines and understory. There is also a wildlife element filled with birds, butterflies, and even an occasional bat. The gardens have also become a major research station, stemming from its therapeutic roots, where plants are grown and analyzed for medicinal use.

GARDEN OPEN: 10 am to 6 pm Sunday–Thursday, 10 am to 8 pm Friday–Saturday.
ADMISSION: $7 adults, $5 seniors and children.

FURTHER INFORMATION FROM:
1 Hope Boulevard, Galveston 77554
(800) 582-4673
www.moodygardens.com

NEARBY SIGHTS OF INTEREST:
Moody Mansion

Moody Gardens' landscaped entrance

TEXAS

GARDEN OPEN: 9 am to 5 pm Tuesday–Sunday, year-round.
ADMISSION: $3.00 adults, $2.50 seniors, $1.50 children.

FURTHER INFORMATION FROM:
8545 South Staples, Corpus Christi 78413
(361) 852-2100

NEARBY SIGHTS OF INTEREST:
Art Museum of South Texas, King Ranch

Plumeria, otherwise known as frangiapani, blooms outdoors at the botanical garden in Corpus Christi.

10 Corpus Christi: Corpus Christi Botanical Garden

LOCATION: STAPLES ROAD, ALONG OSO CREEK, SOUTHWEST OF DOWNTOWN

Lazy Oso Creek winds down the edge of Corpus Christi, cradling it in its elbow, before emptying into the Gulf of Mexico. Although the city has largely ignored the creek, the young but upwardly mobile botanical garden has embraced it whole heartedly. The Corpus Christi Botanical Garden is a small but rapidly growing place. Conservation has been a strong influence in its development thus far and, armed with grants from wetland conservation agencies, it has created a garden along the banks of the Oso. Besides the numerous subtropical bird species, the garden highlights the native mesquite forest. Upland from here in recent years several botanical collections have been developed. The Hibiscus Garden, completed in 1999, showcases 75 varieties of what, since 1957, has been the city's official flower. A new arch-shaped rose garden is laid with brick walkways and raised beds designed by landscape architect Robert Gignac. Within a small greenhouse complex are a surprisingly large collection of orchids (1000 strong) and a more modest display of bromeliads, cycads, and other tropicals. Outside of this structure is a small garden of frangipani, which is moved indoors during the winter. The trails toward the creek begin and end in these central gardens, providing visitors with an opportunity to experience the transition of controlled garden environments to more wild areas—and back again. One recommendation: watch out for occasional alligators.

Biographies

Audubon, John James (1783–1851) Naturalist and artist who traveled the South and other areas to study wildlife, which he immortalized in his illustrated books.

Hopkins, Alden (1905–1960) Landscape architect of Colonial Williamsburg and purveyor of colonial revival gardens in the 1940s and 1950s, including those at Gunston Hall and Elizabethtown.

Innocenti and Webel A New York City landscape architecture firm, popular in the 1930s and 1940s for their work on spectacular residential estates.

Jefferson, Thomas (1743–1826) Besides his political achievements, considered one of the first major architects and landscape architects in the country.

Jekyll [pronounced JEE'kul], Gertrude (1842–1932) Artist and garden designer famous for developing the English cottage garden style, notable for its informal, impressionistic use of color laid against a geometric background.

Olmsted Brothers Landscape architecture firm created by Frederick Law Olmsted, and managed by his son, Frederick Law Olmsted Jr., and nephew and stepson, John Charles Olmsted, after the senior designer's death. Completed more than 3,500 commission between 1898 and 1920.

Olmsted, Frederick Law (1822–1903) The best-known American landscape architect, responsible for Central Park in New York and Boston's "Emerald Necklass," in addition to George Vanderbilt's Biltmore Estate in Asheville, North Carolina.

Olmsted, Frederick Law Jr. (1850–1920) Son of Frederick Law Olmsted, who carried on his successful practice into the twentieth century. Worked on many important residential projects, including the Bok Tower Garden in Florida.

Phillips, William Lyman (1885–1966) Landscape architect who apprenticed with the Olmsted office and then relocated to Florida in the 1930s. Was responsible for the design of Coral Gables, many of the Miami islands, and the Fairchild Tropical Garden.

Shipman, Ellen Biddle (1869–1950) A major figure in early-twentieth-century gardening. In the south she designed the Italian terraces at the Sarah B. Duke Gardens in North Carolina and Longue Vue in New Orleans.

Shurcliff, Arthur (née Shurtleff) (1870–1957) Boston landscape architect who designed Colonial Williamsburg and co-founded the landscape architecture program at Harvard University, the first in the country. He was influential in developing the colonial revival style in the Northeast and mid-Atlantic South.

Glossary

riparian Refers to plants or plant communities that grow on the edges or banks of rivers or lakes.

exedra (Greek) A semicircular outdoor bench with an unusually high back. In ancient Greece and Rome, it was used as a meeting place.

Shakespearean garden A garden composed of herbs and flowers mentioned in the works of William Shakespeare.

succession The natural progress of a forest from meadow to scrub to immature than mature hardwood.

tufa A type of rock with sharp edges and a porous composition, used to stabilize acidic soils. Frequently used in the design of pools and ponds.

Index

Ambaz, Emillio 140–41
Afton Villa 89, 98–100
Agecroft Hall xi, 14–15
Alfred B. Maclay Gardens 112
American Horticultural Society 6
American Rose Center 97
American Rose Society 97
Arlie Gardens 29
Asheville, Botanical Gardens 40
Ashland 42–43
Athens Ladies Garden Club
Atlanta Botanical Garden 76
Atlanta History Center 77–78
Audubon House and Tropical Gardens 129
Audubon, John James 129, 145
Avery Island 108, 109

Bailey, Karen "KB" 13
Bartram, John 1, 81
Bartram, William 81
Baskerville, John 17
Bayless, J. Lyle 109
Bayou Bend 131–32, 142
Bellingrath Gardens 87
Bellingrath, Walter 56, and Bessie Mae Morse 87
Berry, Francis Rhea 82
Berry, Martha 82–83
Bill of Rights 8
Biltmore Estate 25, 36–39
Birmingham Botanical Gardens 84
Bland, Dan 70
Boehme, Edward Marshall 87
Bok, Edward 117–18
Bok Towers viii, 117–18
Boroughs, John 98
Boxerwood Gardens 12–13
Brookgreen Gardens 57
Buck, Charles Austin 118
Burbank, Luther 120
Busch Entertainment Corporation 116

Callaway, Cason and Virginia 73–75
Callaway Gardens 55–56, 72–75
Carter, George 3
Carter, Robert "King" 3
Cave Hill 26, 45–46
Chalfin, Paul 125–26
Chambliss, John 26, 47
Cheek family 48
Cheekwood 48
Clarkson, Elizabeth and Edwin 33–34
Clay, Henry 42–43, 44
Clinton, Hillary Rodham 111
Craig, Gualden, and Davis Architects 74
Civil War ix, 3, 13, 20, 45, 58, 61–62, 131
Coker College 65
Coker family 65
Coker, Miss May 65
Colonial Williamsburg 2, 9, 10, 13, 18–22
Cook, Arthur B. 112
Corpus Christi Botanical Garden 132, 144
Crosby Arboretum 90, 94–96
Crosby, L.O. 95
Crummins, Jim and Mollie 121
Crump, E.H. 53
Crutchfield, Hope 52
Cypress Gardens (South Carolina) 58
Cypress Gardens (Florida) 116–17

Dallas Arboretum and Botanic Garden 131, 134
Dallas Horticulture Center 131, 135
de Monceau, Duhamel 7
Deering, John 125
DeGolyer, Everette Lee 134
Design Consortium 106
Disney, Walt 19
Disney World 22, 89, 94
Dixon Gallery and Gardens 52
Dixon, Margaret and Hugo 52
Dooley, James and Sallie May 17
Dothan Area Botanical Gardens 86
Drayton family 62
Drayton, Reverend John Grimke 62
Duke, Mary 32
Duke, Sarah P. 32
Duke University 25, 32–33
du Pont, Henry F. 132, 142

Edison Estate 120
Edison, Thomas Alva 120
Eliot, Charles 47
Elizabethan Gardens 26, 27
Emery, Lyn 104
Environmental Planning and Design 66
Eureka Springs Gardens 90, 91
Eustis, William and Edith 3

Fairchild, David 127
Fairchild Tropical Garden 111, 127–128
Faulkner, William ix, 115
Farrand, Beatrix 5
Fernbank Science Center ix, 78–79
Fitzgerald, Ben and Mary 85
Flamingo Gardens 123
Fleming, Bryant 48
Ford, Henry 98
Forrester, Nancy ix, 112, 128–29
Fort Worth Botanic Garden 136
Founders Memorial Garden 79–80
French, Daniel Chester 57

Galle, Fred C. 81
Garden Club of Virginia 10
Garvan, Verena 92
Garvan Woodlands Gardens 92
Geiger, John Huling and Lucretia 129
Generalife Gardens 90, 104
Georgia Southern University Botanical Garden 70
Georgia State Botanical Garden 81
Gignac, Robert 144
Gillette, Charles 14–15, 16
Gilliland, Ezra 120
Green, Mynelle Westerfield 93
Green, Paul 31
Green Spring Garden Park 5
Gone With the Wind xi

Harcourt Brace Jovanovich 116
Harrison, Emily 78
Harry P. Leu Gardens 114
Hart, Captain Thomas 65
Haupt, Enid Annenberg 6
Heathcote Botanical Gardens 121
Heery Architects and Engineers 76
Hermitage 49–50
Heyward, Thomas Jr. 64
Heyward-Washington House 64
Hilltop Arboretum 100
Hodges Garden 98
Hogg, Ima 132, 142
Hogg, Jim 142
Hopkins, Alden 2, 9, 10, 14, 145
Hunt, Richard Morris 37–38
Huntington, Archer Milton and Anna 57
Hunstville-Madison County Botanical Garden 83

Innocenti and Webel 14, 27, 43, 145

Jackson, Andrew 49–50
Jackson, Rachel 49–50
Japanese gardens 17, 48, 53, 71, 76, 84, 87, 109, 121, 136, 141
Jasmine Hill Gardens and Outdoor Museum 85
J.C. Raulston Arboretum 30
Jefferson, Joseph 109
Jefferson, Thomas 1, 10, 11–12, 19, 20, 145
Jekyll, Gertrude 5, 145
Johnson, Lady Bird 137
Johnson Outboard 116

INDEX

Jones, Fay 92, 96
Jones, Pembroke 29
Jova, Henri V. 73
Jungle Gardens 108

Kaiser Wilhem 29
Kalmia Gardens of Coker College 65
Kawana, Koichi 53
Kenney, Henry Fletcher 43
Kittredge, William 58
Kuralt, Charles 128

Lacy, Alan 128
Ladies Home Journal, The 117
Lady Bird Johnson Wildflower Center xi, 131, 137–40
Lee, Thomas 13
Lee, Robert E. 13
Le Notre, Andre vii, 59
Leu, Harry P. 92
Lewis and Clark expedition 1, 12
Lexington Cemetery 44
Live Oak Gardens 109
Longue Vue 90, 102–06
Lord and Burnham 79
Lorton Hall 8–9
Louisiana State University 99, 100

Maclay, Alfred B and Louise Fleischman 112
Maclay Gardens 111, 112
Madlinger, George 53
Magnolia Plantation ix, 55, 62–63
Marie Selby Botanical Gardens xi, 111, 119
Marvin, Robert 74
Marx, Roberto Burle 137
Mason, George 8–9
Massee Lane Gardens 71
Maymont 17
Mercer Arboretum 141
Mercer, Thelma and Charles 141
McIlhenny, E.A. 108, 109
Medary, Milton B. 117
Memphis Botanic Garden 53
Middleton, Henry 55, 59–62
Middleton Place ix, 55, 59–62
Mississippi State University 95

Montgomery, Colonel Robert 127
Monticello 1, 10, 11–12
Moody Gardens 143
Moody, Robert L. 143
Morrison, Darrel 56, 78
Mount Vernon xii, 6, 7–8
Mounts Botanical Garden 122
Mounts, Marvin "Red" 122
Munger, Robert 12–13
Muto 17
Mynelle Gardens 93

Nancy Forrester's Secret Garden 112, 128–29
NASA 83
National Trust for Historic Preservation 3
New Orleans Botanical Garden 101
New Orleans Country Club 103
New Orleans Garden District 107
New York Times 47
Noland and Baskerville 17
Norfolk Botanical Garden xi, 2, 23
Norris Hall and Marsh Architects 81
North Carolina Arboretum 25, 41–42
North Carolina Botanical Garden 31
North Carolina State Arboretum 30

Oakhill 82–83
Oatlands Plantation 3
Ochs, Adolph 47
Ogden, Doan 40
Oglethorpe, James 68–69
Oldenwald, Neil 119
Olmsted Company 117, 145
Olmsted, Frederick Law 19, 25, 37–39, 41, 127, 145
Olmsted, Frederick Law Jr. 117, 145

Parker, Herb 67
Parton, Dolly 133
Phillips, William Lyman 117–18, 127, 145
Pinewood 96
plantations ix, 3, 6, 7–9, 11–12, 13–14, 58, 59–62, 62–63, 65, 89, 98–100
Platt, William and Geoffrey 103–06
Pope, Dick 116

Raleigh, Sir Walter 27
Raulston, J.C. 30
Richards, Kerry and Christiana 115
Rip Van Winkle Gardens 109
River Farm 6
Riverbanks Botanical Garden 66
Riverbanks Zoo 66
Reeves, Joel 74
Reflection Riding 26, 47
Revolutionary War 7
Roberts, Edgerton 17
Rockefeller, John D. Jr. 13, 19
Rosenwald, Edith 103

Saint-Gaudens, Augustus 57
San Antonio Botanical Garden 140–41
Sanders, Colonel 46
Sarah P. Duke Gardens 25, 32–33
Savannah Gardens 68–69
Scarritt-Bennet Center 51
Schadow, Johann Rudolph 61
Sears and Roebuck 103
Selby, Marie and William 119
Shelburne Farms 37
Shinn, Bruce 40
Shipman, Ellen Biddle 32, 90, 103–06, 145
Shurcliff, Arthur 13, 19–22, 145
Shutze, Philip Trammell 77–78
Siani, Alfredo 3
Smith, Emory 100
South Carolina Botanical Garden 67
Starke, Barry 17
Staub, John 142
Stern, Edgar 103–06
Stevens, John 71
Stratford Hall 13–14
Strother, Dave 71
Suarez, Diego 125–26

Tabasco 108

Tennessee River Garden 46
Thompson, Thomas 23
Topel, R.A. 29
Trimble, Morrell and Genevieve 89, 98–100
Tryon Palace 26, 28
Tryon, William 28
Tull, Jethro 7
Tyler Rose Garden 131, 133
Twentieth Century Gardens 92

United Methodist Council of Churches 51
University of Arkansas 92
University of Georgia 81
University of North Carolina 41
University of North Carolina at Asheville 40
University of Virginia 1, 10, 11
University of Virginia Pavilion Gardens 10

Vanderbilt family 37–39
Vanderbilt, George 25, 37–39, 41
van Valkenburgh, Michael 48
Versailles vii
Virginia Declaration of Rights 8
Virginia House 16
Vizcaya 111, 124–26

Washington, George 1, 6, 7–8, 64
Wedell, Alexander and Virginia 16
Wheelock, Morgan 134
William and Mary College 19
Williams T.C. 14, 16
Wilson, Ernest Henry 81
Wing Haven Gardens & Bird Sanctuary 33–34
Winkler Botanical Preserve ix, 4
Winterthur 142
Wirth, Tom 75
World of Orchids 111, 115
Wray, Floyd and Jane 123
Wu, Kingsley 136

Yasui, Koishi 141
Young, Arthur 7

Acknowledgments

A medal of honor to my family, Lani and Sadie, for putting up with me and offering crucial criticism and continual support. Hats off to the parents, Gary and Frankie Bennett, and parents-in-law, Barry and Marilyn Bevacqua. Landscape architects, garden designers, and directors of several gardens offered inspiration and assistance beyond compare, among these are Kent Brinkley at Colonial Williamsburg and Bob Brzusek at Crosby Arboretum. My source for the discussion of Le Nôtre in the foreword was Michel Conan, at Dumbarton Oaks. *Gracias* friends.

Photograph credits

i, 26–39 The Biltmore Company
xii, 11, 68–69 Jan Cigliano
2, 17 Richard Cheek
3 Ron Blount, National Trust for Historic Preservation
5 Brenda Skarphol
6 tphalen
10 Walter Smalling Jr.
13 Christopher Cunningham, Stratford Hall Plantation
15 Dwight Dike
16 Ping Amranand
18–22 Colonial Williamsburg Foundation
33 Edmund Albrecht
35 Jim Legget
43 K. Colebark
51 Jenna Bivens
76 Thomas G. Ness
77 Atlanta History Center
80–81 Carol and Hugh Nourse
97 Joyce True
113 Dick Dietrich
122–126 Longue Vue
127 Steven Forster
129 Dan Dry & Associates
130 Marion L. Buerger
142 Museum of Fine Arts, Houston; Bayou Bend Collection and Gardens